Ess Skills for Reading Success:

Strategies for Reading Comprehension and Test Taking *Revised*

by Howard I. Berrent, Ph.D. and Edward R. Nasello

RALLY! EDUCATION, LLC

Glen Head, New York

We're all about student success!

ISBN 1-58380-996-1

Published 2004. Fourth Edition 2006
Printed in the U.S.A.

Cover Designer: Jean-Paul Vest
Book Designer: Lori Harley
Editor: Pat Keiserman
Illustrator, pages 6, 22, 76, 87: Donna Stackhouse

RALLY! EDUCATION
22 Railroad Avenue
Glen Head, NY 11545
tel 888·99·RALLY
fax 516·671·7900
www.RALLYEDUCATION.com

Essential Skills for Reading Success
Strategies for Reading Comprehension and Test Taking

Table of Contents

Introduction

Welcome to ***Essential Skills for Reading Success:*** *Strategies for Reading Comprehension and Test Taking.* Being a successful reader means that you understand what you read. There are fourteen important skills you need to be a great reader. This book teaches you strategies, which are ways to use the skills when you read. It also teaches you how to answer reading comprehension questions on tests.

Essential Skills for Reading Success has different kinds of reading selections and different types of questions. You will read passages that are poems, and other passages that give you information, tell a story, or explain how to do something. You will be asked multiple-choice questions and questions that require you to write out an answer. When you finish this book you will be a better reader and a better test taker.

Essential Skills for Reading Success is made up of two parts:

Part A will teach you the essential reading comprehension skills one-by-one.

Part B will teach you the essential reading comprehension skills all together.

Throughout the book, we will provide *Strategies, Hints,* and *Reminders* to make learning easier for you. First we will model what we teach. Then we will guide you. Finally we will provide you with independent study to try on your own what you have learned.

When you finish ***Essential Skills for Reading Success*** you will be a better reader and a better test taker.

4

PART A

The 14 Essential Skills for Reading Success

One-by-One

Each of the fourteen reading comprehension skills are taught one-by-one in this part. First you will read a passage. You will then be asked some questions.

In **Modeled Instruction,** we will teach you a strategy that you can use to answer each question. Then we will explain each of the answer choices. We will show you why some of the choices are not correct. We will explain why the correct choice is the answer.

In **Guided Instruction,** we will provide *Hints* for you on how to answer the question. The first question will be multiple-choice. The second question will ask you to write out the answer.

In **Independent Study,** you will be on your own. You will answer multiple-choice and open-ended questions.

1 **Recall Facts and Details**

2 **Identify Main Idea**

3 **Identify Sequence**

4 **Analyze Language and Vocabulary**

5 **Analyze Character, Plot, and Setting**

6 **Recognize Cause and Effect**

7 **Compare and Contrast**

8 **Distinguish Fact from Opinion**

9 **Predict Outcomes**

10 **Draw Conclusions**

11 **Make Inferences**

12 **Analyze Point of View and Purpose**

13 **Identify Literary Forms and Sources of Information**

14 **Apply Prior Knowledge**

A Skill 1: Recall Facts and Details

When answering questions based on a passage you must be able to remember information. These facts and details can be found in the passage. Often you will need to read the passage a second time to find the information you need to answer a question.

Directions: Read the passage below. The passage is followed by questions that can be answered by recalling facts and details. Use this passage to answer all the questions on pages 7–9.

Just the Way She Likes It

Emily's sister, Jennifer, had left for college last week, and Emily was moving into her room. Finally, she wouldn't have to share a room with her younger sister. Kathy was just five years old, and they had shared a room since she was born. It had always been crowded in there, and Emily was constantly tripping over Kathy's toys. There was no privacy, and the whole situation was often frustrating.

Before she moved her bed and bureau into her new room, Emily had to vacuum and dust it. She hauled the heavy vacuum cleaner up the stairs and proceeded to suck up all the remnants from Jennifer's life. Ginger, the family cat, loved sitting in this room's bay window, so orange hair covered the floor. Suddenly,

the vacuum cleaner coughed and sputtered. Emily stopped and pulled a hairclip out of the hose. It was the blue glittery one that Jennifer had been missing since last summer. Emily felt sad thinking about Jennifer and realized she missed her big sister already. Gazing around the room, Emily remembered all the times Jennifer had played games with her in here. Jennifer had always helped Emily with her homework and had advised her about high school and what to expect. She was a good sister. Now, Emily would be queen of this castle, but first, she had to make the place hers.

When Emily finished cleaning the empty room, she and her father hauled in her furniture. She had a difficult time figuring out where she wanted to situate the bed.

First, she tried it over by the window, but she realized that the sun would be shining directly on her face in the early morning, so that wouldn't work. Then, they moved the bed to the far corner, but that left no room for her bureau and comfy chair.

In the end, they put her bed in the exact spot where Jennifer's had been. They positioned the bureau next to the closet and placed the chair in the corner. At last it was beginning to look just the way Emily had envisioned it. She spent the rest of the morning putting away her clothes.

While Emily was in her old room getting the last of her belongings, Kathy came in and started messing up her piles of clothes. Usually, Emily would have told her to scram, but today she was a little more patient with her younger sister. She let Kathy look through the stack of sweaters that didn't fit her anymore, and even let her borrow the red and purple one with the flowers on it. When she made the last trip with her belongings, another pang of sadness tore through Emily, and she decided it hadn't been all bad sharing a room with Kathy. She would miss their late-night giggle sessions.

After lunch, Emily started the most enjoyable part of her project. She removed Jennifer's old blue curtains and hung the bright yellow ones that her mother had helped her sew over the summer. Emily loved yellow because it was so sunny and happy, and the curtains matched her daisy-covered comforter. Next, she looked at the bare walls where faint traces indicated where Jennifer's posters had hung. Emily decided to hang her two favorite photographs over the bureau. One pictured the beach house where her family spent their summers. The rising sun backlit the quaint cottage, and the dune grass swayed in the morning breeze. The photograph brought back all the happy vacation memories. She had shot that photo herself. The other was a close-up of Emily and her best friend, Melissa, whispering to each other beneath the maple tree in the backyard. Looking at it created a feeling of safety and peace in Emily. Lastly, Emily put up a bulletin board above her chair, and tacked on things like her class schedule and her friends' phone numbers. When Emily finally sat down and surveyed her realm, she felt truly at home.

Modeled Instruction

Directions: Below is an example of a question that can be answered by recalling facts and details. Follow the strategy that is explained to help choose the correct answer.

---

1 Who is Emily's younger sister?

Ⓐ Kathy

Ⓑ Jennifer

Ⓒ Melissa

Ⓓ Ginger

Strategy: Use key words from the question to help you find where to look in the passage to find the answer. The key words for this question are "Emily's younger sister". Read the parts of the passage that contain the key words. You should be able to find the facts and details that tell you what the correct answer is.

Use this strategy to decide which answer is correct.

Ⓐ **Kathy**

The key words "younger sister" and the name "Kathy" can be found in both the first and the fifth paragraph. A sentence in the first paragraph states that Emily won't have to share a room with her younger sister, Kathy. Therefore, *choice "A" must be the correct answer.*

Ⓒ **Melissa**

The name Melissa can be found in the last paragraph. However, the key words "younger sister" cannot be found in this paragraph. Details in the passage state that Melissa is Emily's best friend, not her sister. Therefore, *choice "C" cannot be the correct answer.*

Ⓑ **Jennifer**

The key word "sister" and the name "Jennifer" can be found in both the first and the second paragraph. Details tell you that Jennifer is Emily's older sister, not her younger sister. Therefore, *choice "B" cannot be correct.*

Ⓓ **Ginger**

The name Ginger can be found in the second paragraph. Details tell you that Ginger is the family cat, and therefore, *choice "D" is not the correct answer.*

Guided Instruction

Directions: Use the hints provided to answer the questions below. For question 2, you must choose the correct answer. For question 3, you will need to write out your answer.

---

2 **What will Emily miss about sharing a room with her little sister?**

- (A) playing with her dollhouse
- (B) sharing clothing with her
- (C) their late-night giggle sessions
- (D) her advice about high school

Hint: Use the key words "miss" and "Kathy" to help find where the answer can be found. Read the part of the passage with these key words carefully to find the details needed to answer the question.

---

3 **When did Kathy look through Emily's sweaters?**

_____

_____

_____

_____

_____

_____

_____

_____

_____

_____

_____

_____

_____

_____

_____

_____

_____

_____

Hint: The fifth paragraph contains the key word "sweaters." It also contains the words "Emily," "Kathy," and "look through." Read this paragraph to find the details needed to answer the question.

Independent Study

Directions: Answer the following questions on your own. For questions 4, 5, and 6, choose the correct answer. For question 7, you must write out your answer.

4 Which sweater did Emily lend to Kathy?

Ⓐ the red and purple one

Ⓑ the bright yellow one

Ⓒ the old blue one

Ⓓ the one with a tear

5 How did Emily situate the bed?

Ⓐ under the window

Ⓑ next to the closet

Ⓒ in the same place as Jennifer

Ⓓ by the door to the bedroom

6 How did Emily get curtains for her new room?

Ⓐ She and her mother made them.

Ⓑ She purchased them at the store.

Ⓒ She took curtains from her old room.

Ⓓ She used Jennifer's old curtains.

7 Why does Emily like the two photographs she puts on her walls?

_____

_____

_____

_____

_____

_____

_____

_____

_____

_____

_____

_____

Skill 2: Identify Main Idea

The main idea is what the whole passage is about. To identify the main idea of a passage, you must think about all of the information in the passage. When a passage tells about more than one thing you must ask yourself what it is mostly about. Some questions may ask you to tell the main idea of a paragraph or a sentence. To answer those questions you only need to think about what the paragraph or sentence is about.

Directions: Read the passage below. The passage is followed by questions that can be answered by identifying main ideas. Use this passage to answer all the questions on pages 11–13.

Brazil

1   South America is made up of many different countries. The largest is Brazil, which borders most of the other countries in South America. Some of the countries bordering Brazil are Venezuela and Columbia on the north, Peru and Bolivia on the west, and Uruguay to the south. The Atlantic Ocean is on Brazil's east coast, and the country has some of the world's most beautiful beaches.

2   Even though Brazil has more land than the rest of the South American countries combined, much of it is jungle where few people can live. Most of Brazil's population lives along the coast in large cities like São Paulo and Río de Janeiro. Unlike most of Brazil's other major cities, Brasília, the capital, is in the less populated middle section of the country. The government chose this location to encourage people to move there.

3   The Portuguese navigator, Pedro Alvares Cabral, discovered Brazil in 1500. From then on, Brazil was under Portuguese rule. When Napoleon invaded Portugal in the early 1800s, the king fled to Brazil and ruled there for years. Then, in 1812, Brazil became independent. Dom Pedro I became the first Emperor of Brazil. He was succeeded by his son, Dom Pedro II. He ruled until 1889, when Brazil became a republic. In the seventeenth century, Brazil was the world's largest sugar producer. Soon, gold and diamonds replaced sugar. By the nineteenth century, coffee was Brazil's major moneymaker and still is today.

4   The 170 million people of Brazil are a combination of many different nationalities. The Portuguese intermarried with the native people and the African slaves that were brought to Brazil. Later, Brazil's resources attracted the French and the Dutch to the northeast area of the country. Then, during the nineteenth century, Germans, Italians, Polish and Japanese came to Brazil. As a result Brazilians may be one of the most racially mixed people of the world.

5   Brazil's national language is Portuguese, but it is very different from the language that is spoken in Portugal. Many people of Brazil say they speak "Brazilian." While some people in Brazil are very wealthy, Brazil also has a great deal of poverty. Families, including grandparents and other relatives, often have to live together in overcrowded, rundown housing.

6   Children in Brazil are educated at either public or private schools. Children are supposed to attend school until they are fourteen years of age, but that requirement is not always strictly enforced. Attendance is often poor because travel is difficult and schools are overcrowded. Many families live in poverty, so children often leave school to get work.

7   Brazilians are known as people who enjoy life to its fullest, and one of the national passions is soccer. Pele, the most famous soccer player in the world, was born in Brazil in 1940. He began playing in the major leagues when he was just fifteen years old. One year later he joined the Brazilian National Team, leading them to World Cup victory in 1958. Pele's physical strength, amazing ball skills, and natural ability enabled him to score 1,281 goals during his career.

8   Brazilian people are also famous for their Carnaval, which was first held in 1641. This national party can be traced back to ancient Roman and Greek celebrations of spring. Carnaval festivities are held from Saturday through Tuesday, and longer in some cities. Brazil's culture and people are celebrated as the population dresses up in costumes to dance in the street. Samba is the most popular music pulsing through the air, as thousands dance to its beat in the world's largest parade.

Modeled Instruction

Directions: Below is an example of a question that can be answered by identifying the main idea of the passage. Follow the strategy that is explained to help choose the correct answer.

---

1   What would be the best title for this passage?

Ⓐ "Brazilian Celebrations"

Ⓑ "Cities on the Beach"

Ⓒ "Interesting Bits about Brazil"

Ⓓ "South American Countries"

Strategy: A good title can tell a reader the main idea of a passage. You need to think about all of the information you read to tell what the main idea of the passage is. Ask yourself, "What is the passage mostly about?"

Use this strategy to decide which answer is correct.

Ⓐ **"Brazilian Celebrations"**

The passage does give information about the Brazilian Carnaval, but only in the eighth paragraph. Since the passage also gives details about the land and cities of Brazil, *choice "A" cannot be correct.*

Ⓑ **"Cities on the Beach"**

In the first paragraph, it is stated that Brazil has beautiful beaches, but no details are given. Since the passage does not discuss beach cities, *choice "B" cannot be correct.*

Ⓒ **"Interesting Bits about Brazil"**

Brazil is mentioned in every paragraph of the passage. Each paragraph gives facts and details about the country. Since the passage is mostly about the country of Brazil, *choice "C" must be the correct answer.*

Ⓓ **"South American Countries"**

The first paragraph does list other countries in South America, but only to tell how they border Brazil. Most of the details in the rest of the passage are about Brazil. Since there is not much information given about the other countries, *choice "D" cannot be correct.*

Guided Instruction

Directions: Use the hints provided to answer the questions below. For question 2, you must choose the correct answer. For question 3, you will need to write out your answer.

---

2 The third paragraph in the passage tells mostly about—

(A) the coast of Brazil

(B) the history of Brazil

(C) the countries that border Brazil

(D) the land and culture of Brazil

Hint: To answer this question you need to look only at the third paragraph. Think about what important facts can be found in this paragraph. Ask yourself what most of these facts tell you about.

---

3 What is the fourth paragraph mostly about?

_____

_____

_____

_____

_____

_____

_____

_____

_____

_____

_____

_____

_____

_____

_____

_____

_____

Hint: Think about the facts and details that are given in the fourth paragraph. What are all the details describing? What are these facts and details telling you about? This is the main idea. Include this information in your answer.

Independent Study

Directions: Answer the following questions on your own. For questions 4, 5, and 6, choose the correct answer. For question 7, you must write out your answer.

4 **What is this passage mostly about?**

(A) Carnaval and Pele

(B) the Brazilian language

(C) the most famous Portuguese explorers

(D) the largest country in South America

5 **What is main idea of the sixth paragraph in the passage?**

(A) Brazilian people are a mix of many nationalities

(B) Brazil celebrates Carnaval for four days

(C) Brazil's system of education

(D) Brazil's interesting sights

6 **Which fact below would fit best in the first paragraph of the passage?**

(A) Guyana borders Brazil to the north.

(B) Porto Allegre and Reafe are cities in Brazil.

(C) Farm land makes up ten percent of Brazil.

(D) Carnaval is a celebration of spring.

7 **Write your own summary about the passage. Remember to include the main idea of each paragraph in your summary.**

_____

_____

_____

_____

_____
_____
_____
_____
_____
_____
_____
_____
_____
_____
_____

Skill 3: Identify Sequence

To identify sequence means to be able to place information or things that have happened in the correct order. To answer questions about sequence you must read the passage to find out when actions or events occur. You must be able to find out at what point in time something happened.

Directions: Read the passage below. The passage is followed by questions that can be answered by identifying sequence. Use this passage to answer all the questions on pages 15–17.

A Vacation Destination

Visit the National Aquarium This Summer

~ Enjoy Fantastic Shows ~
~ Dive into Underwater Tours ~ Explore the Touch Tank ~

Aquarium Hours: *(Show times below)*	**Tours and Touch Tank**	**Exhibits**
Sunday through Thursday	9:00 A.M.–6:00 P.M.	9:00 A.M.–8:00 P.M.
Friday and Saturday	9:00 A.M.–8:00 P.M.	9:00 A.M.–10:00 P.M.

Directions: Take I-91 South to Exit 53 | Take I-495 North to the Harbor | Exit and turn left | At the 6th light, turn right onto Canal Street | Go four blocks and the National Aquarium is on the left

The Shark Shop *Hours: 10:00 A.M. until the aquarium closes.*
Take the world of the sea home with you by visiting the gift store, which is located on the upper level of the Marine Mammal Pavilion. Merchandise includes T-shirts, jewelry, books, and other fascinating mementos of your visit.

Feeding Frenzy Food Court Goldfish not on the menu! *Hours: 10:00 A.M.–7:00 P.M.*

"Early Seagull" lunch specials	"Early Seagull" dinner specials
11:30 A.M.–12:30 A.M.	5:00 P.M.–6:00 P.M.

Daily Shows: *(All are thirty minutes long.)*

Bewitching Seahorses	9:30 A.M.	Enjoy an informative and entertaining in-depth look at ten different species of seahorses, including Spotted, Thorny, Hedgehog, Speckled, and Pot Bellied. Did you know that only male seahorses can have babies?
Shark Showcase	11:00 A.M.	Shiver and shake from the snug safety of your seat as you get a close-up view of sharks during this incredible performance!
Dolphin Acrobatics	1:30 P.M.	They leap, twist, and dive in an astounding display of power and grace. Sit up front if you want to enjoy a cooling splash!
Penguin Parade	4:45 P.M.	Watch these water birds waddle on land and romp in their pool. The penguins are garbed in elegant tuxedos, but you can come in casual attire.

The sea lions slither and slide, catch fish, and play ball. Come and see Big Bob, the largest of them all, perform his stunts in an amazing finale.

Questions? Concerns? Visit the main office on the upper level. Open every day from 8:30 A.M.–4:30 P.M.

Modeled Instruction

Directions: Below is an example of a question that can be answered by identifying the sequence of events. Follow the strategy that is explained to help choose the correct answer.

---

1 Which show starts before the "Early Seagull" lunch special begins and after the gift shop opens?

Ⓐ Penguin Parade

Ⓑ Bewitching Seahorses

Ⓒ Dolphin Acrobatics

Ⓓ Shark Showcase

Strategy: To answer questions that require identifying sequence it can be helpful to create a timeline. Read the passage and look for key times to help you determine when things happen. You should complete this timeline before you answer the question.

9:30 A.M. _____

_____

_____

_____

_____

_____

_____

Use this strategy to decide which answer is correct.

Ⓐ **Penguin Parade**

The Penguin Parade begins at 4:45 P.M. Since this show begins after the lunch special begins, *choice "A" is not the correct choice.*

Ⓒ **Dolphin Acrobatics**

This starts at 1:30 P.M., which is after the lunch special begins at 11:30 A.M. and after the gift shop opens at 10:00 A.M. Therefore, *choice "C" cannot be the correct choice.*

Ⓑ **Bewitching Seahorses**

The seahorse show begins before the gift shop opens, not after the gift shop opens. Therefore, *choice "B" cannot be the correct choice.*

Ⓓ **Shark Showcase**

This show begins at 11:00 A.M. This is after the gift shop opens at 10:00 A.M. and before the "Early Seagull" lunch special begins at 11:30 A.M. Therefore, *choice "D" is the correct answer.*

Guided Instruction

Directions: Use the hints provided to answer the questions below. For question 2, you must choose the correct answer. For question 3, you will need to write out your answer.

---

2 **Which of the following opens first?**

(A) the aquarium

(B) the main office

(C) the gift shop

(D) the food court

Hint: Look at the information given to find the time at which each event occurs. Use this information in your timeline of events to answer this question. Ask yourself which event occurs first.

---

3 **List three things you could do at the aquarium if you arrived at 1:00 P.M. on Saturday.**

_____

_____

_____

_____

_____

_____

_____

_____

_____

_____

_____

_____

_____

_____

_____

_____

_____

_____

_____

_____

Hint: Identify all of the events that begin after 1:00 P.M. Be sure to consider things you could do besides seeing shows.

Independent Study

Directions: Answer the following questions on your own. For questions 4, 5, and 6, choose the correct answer. For question 7, you must write out your answer.

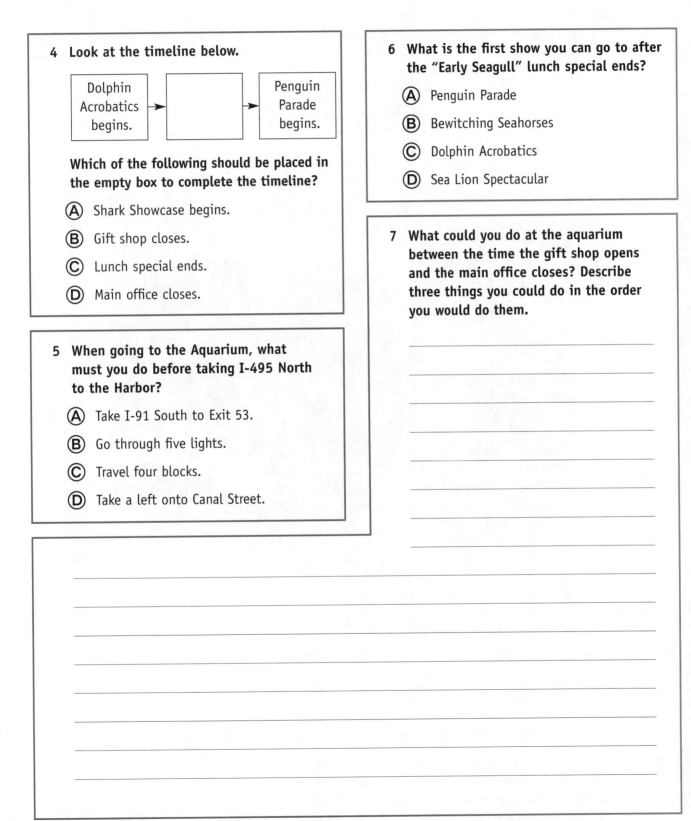

4   Look at the timeline below.

| Dolphin Acrobatics begins. | → | | → | Penguin Parade begins. |

Which of the following should be placed in the empty box to complete the timeline?

Ⓐ Shark Showcase begins.

Ⓑ Gift shop closes.

Ⓒ Lunch special ends.

Ⓓ Main office closes.

5   When going to the Aquarium, what must you do before taking I-495 North to the Harbor?

Ⓐ Take I-91 South to Exit 53.

Ⓑ Go through five lights.

Ⓒ Travel four blocks.

Ⓓ Take a left onto Canal Street.

6   What is the first show you can go to after the "Early Seagull" lunch special ends?

Ⓐ Penguin Parade

Ⓑ Bewitching Seahorses

Ⓒ Dolphin Acrobatics

Ⓓ Sea Lion Spectacular

7   What could you do at the aquarium between the time the gift shop opens and the main office closes? Describe three things you could do in the order you would do them.

_____

_____

_____

_____

_____

_____

_____

_____

_____

_____

_____

_____

_____

_____

Skill 4: Analyze Language and Vocabulary

To analyze language you must look at the words, phrases, and sentences and how they are used in a passage. Sometimes you will be asked to tell what the words mean. At other times you may need to explain how words are used to express ideas or to tell a story.

Directions: Read the poem below. The poem is followed by questions that can be answered by analyzing words, phrases, and sentences. Use this poem to answer all the questions on pages 19–21.

Sea-Fever

by John Masefield (1878-1967)

1   I must down to the seas again, to the lonely sea and the sky,
2   And all I ask is a tall ship and a star to steer her by,
3   And the wheel's kick and the wind's song and the white sail's shaking,
4   And a grey mist on the sea's face, and a grey dawn breaking.

5   I must down to the seas again, for the call of the running tide
6   Is a wild call and a clear call that may not be denied;
7   And all I ask is a windy day with the white clouds flying,
8   And the flung spray and the blown *spume,* and the sea-gulls crying.

9   I must down to the seas again, to the *vagrant* gypsy life,
10 To the gull's way and the whale's way where the wind's like a whetted knife;
11 And all I ask is a merry yarn from a laughing fellow-rover
12 And quiet sleep and a sweet dream when the long *trick's* over.

Modeled Instruction

Directions: Below is an example of a question that can be answered by analyzing language in the passage. Follow the strategy that is explained to help choose the correct answer.

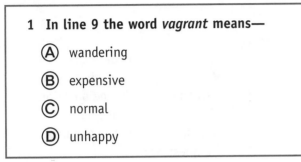

1 In line 9 the word *vagrant* means—

Ⓐ wandering

Ⓑ expensive

Ⓒ normal

Ⓓ unhappy

Strategy: Thinking about how a word is used in a sentence can help you to understand its meaning. Some words in a sentence can give you clues about the meaning of other words. Sometimes you may need to look at a few sentences and how they fit together in order to discover the meaning of a word. The word vagrant is in the last stanza, or part, of the poem.

Use this strategy to decide which answer is correct.

 Ⓐ **wandering**

The word "vagrant" is followed by the word "gypsy," a person from a wandering people. The poem also mentions that this is the life of the gull and the whale, animals that are constantly moving from one place to another. Since "wandering" seems to be the best meaning for the word, *choice "A" must be the correct answer.*

 Ⓒ **normal**

The poem tells about the speaker's intense love of life on the sea. There are no words or sentences that suggest this love is the normal way of life for most people. Therefore, *choice "C" does not appear to give the best possible meaning for the word.*

think Ⓑ **expensive**

There is no mention in the poem of the cost of anything. The poet talks about the sky and the sea, not about things that would cost money. Therefore, *choice "B" is not correct.*

 Ⓓ **unhappy**

This poem tells about the speaker's positive feelings for the sea. Details such as "merry," "laughing" and "sweet" are all happy descriptions, not unhappy ones. Therefore, *choice "D" is not correct.*

Guided Instruction

Directions: Use the hints provided to answer the questions below. For question 2, you must choose the correct answer. For question 3, you will need to write out your answer.

2 The phrase "where the wind's like a whetted knife" suggests—

(A) the wind is silver and shiny

(B) the wind looks like a knife

(C) the wind is sharp and cutting

(D) the wind can be used like a knife

Hint: Compare the group of words in each answer with the words in the question. Which answer choice has the same meaning as the words in the question?

3 What do you think the phrase "a merry yarn from a laughing fellow-rover" means?

_____

_____

_____

_____

_____

_____

_____

_____

_____

_____

_____

_____

_____

_____

_____

_____

_____

Hint: Read the part of the poem where this phrase is used. What do the details tell you about what this phrase might mean?

Independent Study

Directions: Answer the following questions on your own. For questions 4, 5, and 6, choose the correct answer. For question 7, you must write out your answer.

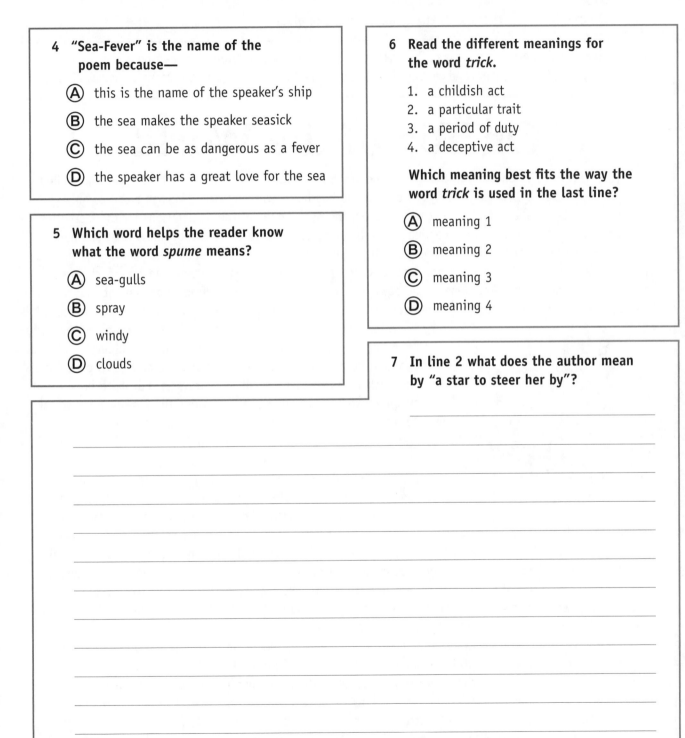

4 "Sea-Fever" is the name of the poem because—

Ⓐ this is the name of the speaker's ship

Ⓑ the sea makes the speaker seasick

Ⓒ the sea can be as dangerous as a fever

Ⓓ the speaker has a great love for the sea

5 Which word helps the reader know what the word *spume* means?

Ⓐ sea-gulls

Ⓑ spray

Ⓒ windy

Ⓓ clouds

6 Read the different meanings for the word *trick*.

1. a childish act
2. a particular trait
3. a period of duty
4. a deceptive act

Which meaning best fits the way the word *trick* is used in the last line?

Ⓐ meaning 1

Ⓑ meaning 2

Ⓒ meaning 3

Ⓓ meaning 4

7 In line 2 what does the author mean by "a star to steer her by"?

Skill 5: Analyze Character, Plot, and Setting

To analyze character, plot, and setting you must be able to describe each one based on information in the passage.

CHARACTER	**who** the passage is about
PLOT	**what** the passage is about
SETTING	**where** and **when** the events take place

Directions: Read the passage below. The passage is followed by questions that can be answered by analyzing the characters, plot, and setting. Use this passage to answer all the questions on pages 23–25.

On Top of the World

When the sun peeked through the blinds and warmed her face, Elizabeth opened her eyes and smiled. Today was the big day, so she jumped out of bed and hustled downstairs. There was so much to do!

At breakfast Elizabeth and her mother discussed the final details of the preparations for the festivities. This afternoon all her friends were coming to her birthday party, and little did they know what she had planned for them. After a hasty breakfast, Elizabeth went to get dressed. When she returned it was time to bake her favorite yellow cake with chocolate frosting. She liked the creamy batter almost as much as the baked cake, so she always left some in the bowl to lick. "I'll never understand how you can eat that raw batter," said her mother. "Don't eat too much of it, Elizabeth. You don't want to get a stomachache today."

After they put the cake in the oven, Elizabeth prepared the party favor bags. Soaring mountains were pictured on the outside of each bag, as well as a guest's name. She filled the bags with chocolates and stickers, as well as a small picture frame. Elizabeth hoped that everyone would insert one of the pictures that she planned to take during her party. When the favor bags were completed, Elizabeth planned to place them on the foyer table in the hallway, so that no one would forget her bag on her departure.

Elizabeth then had a quick lunch with her father in the computer room. While she munched on her tuna fish sandwich, her father instructed her on how to use his digital camera. The telephoto option was an essential feature that would enable Elizabeth to get a close-up picture of each of her friends. Elizabeth's father then showed her how to download and print the pictures she would take.

It was almost time, so Elizabeth went outside and sat on the front porch, waiting anxiously. Her guests were supposed to arrive at two this afternoon. The truck was scheduled to be here at one o'clock, but it was already ten after. Just then, Elizabeth heard something rumbling up the hill. "It's here!" she yelled. Elizabeth's dad came out to help the men unload and set up the synthetic rock wall in the backyard.

Elizabeth's guests started to arrive and, without exception, they were both startled and delighted by the size of the man-made mountain looming in front of them. Soon each would take turns climbing the gigantic wall. When all the birthday guests were present, the rock climbing instructor, Mr. DeAngelis, told them about the equipment they would use and how to proceed. He showed them the helmet they would wear and the harness, which would be attached around their waists. This safety precaution allowed them to climb without the possibility of falling to the ground. If anyone were to lose her grip, the harness would stop the fall. Then, Mr. DeAngelis confirmed that all the girls had worn stiff, athletic-type shoes as they had been instructed to do on their invitations. Lastly, he directed each girl to cover her hands with the chalk he provided, because it would improve her grip by absorbing the sweat. His final piece of advice was to concentrate and to break down the climb into stages. Plan the first stage, achieve that goal, and go on to the next stage, until you reach the top.

Elizabeth was the first to attack the challenge. She donned the harness, adjusted the helmet, and chalked her hands. Then, she began the ascent. One deliberate step at a time, Elizabeth scaled her way up to the peak. When she reached the summit, she looked down at her audience below. Her smile revealed the immense sense of accomplishment she felt. Then, she remembered to wave at her father, who clicked a picture of her. Afterward, she rappelled down while her friends clapped and cheered. As each of her friends took her turn, Elizabeth snapped a picture of each of them at the pinnacle of her birthday mountain.

Then the girls settled down for cake and ice cream at the picnic table in the backyard, chattering the whole while about the rock-climbing escapade. All agreed that it was exciting and most of all, it was different. While her birthday guests enjoyed the party, Elizabeth stole back inside the house and hurried to the computer room, where she printed photographs for her friends' party bags.

That night, after her friends had departed and the rock-climbing wall had been dismantled and taken away, Elizabeth lay in her bed and smiled as she reviewed the day. Just before drifting to sleep, she looked at her picture. There she was waving from the top of her birthday mountain. She felt on top of the world.

Modeled Instruction

Directions: Below is an example of a question that can be answered by analyzing character, plot, and setting in the passage. Follow the strategy that is explained to help choose the correct answer.

> **1** Where in Elizabeth's house does the story NOT take place?
>
> Ⓐ in the kitchen
>
> Ⓑ in the hallway
>
> Ⓒ in the backyard
>
> Ⓓ in the computer room

Strategy: To analyze character, plot and setting it can be helpful to organize details in a story. A story map uses a series of boxes and arrows to show what happens in the story. It shows who does what. It can also show where events in the story take place. This question is asking you about the setting.

Use this strategy to decide which answer is correct.

Ⓐ **in the kitchen**

The kitchen is the room where Elizabeth and her mother eat breakfast and bake the birthday cake. Therefore, *choice "A" cannot be the correct choice.*

Ⓒ **in the backyard**

Different events in the story occur in different places. When the girls climb the rock wall and eat cake, they are in the backyard. Therefore, *choice "C" cannot be the correct choice.*

Ⓑ **in the hallway**

One part of the story does mention that Elizabeth plans to place the favor bags in the hallway. However, no action in the story actually takes place in this room. Therefore, *choice "B" must be the correct answer.*

Ⓓ **in the computer room**

Different parts of the story take place in different rooms of Elizabeth's house. Elizabeth learns about the digital camera in the computer room. Therefore, *choice "D" cannot be the correct choice.*

Guided Instruction

Directions: Use the hints provided to answer the questions below. For question 2, you must choose the correct answer. For question 3, you will need to write out your answer.

2 **From reading the passage you can tell that Elizabeth's mother—**

Ⓐ doesn't like climbing

Ⓑ enjoys baking in the kitchen

Ⓒ is excited about the party

Ⓓ doesn't like raw cake mix

Hint: Think about Elizabeth's mother's actions and words in the story. The things that a character does or says can tell you a lot about him or her. This is a character question.

3 **Summarize what this passage is about. Explain what happens in the beginning, the middle, and the end of the story. This is a plot question.**

_____

_____

_____

_____

_____

_____

_____

_____

_____

_____

_____

_____

_____

_____

_____

_____

_____

_____

Hint: To summarize the plot of a passage you need to explain only about important details and events. Think about what information would be important to know about.

Who is the story about?	**What** is the story about?
When does the story take place?	**Where** does the story take place?

Independent Study

Directions: Answer the following questions on your own. For questions 4, 5, and 6, choose the correct answer. For question 7, you must write out your answer.

4 Elizabeth can best be described as—

- Ⓐ timid
- Ⓑ intelligent
- Ⓒ organized
- Ⓓ impatient

5 Where is Elizabeth when the story begins and ends?

- Ⓐ in her bedroom
- Ⓑ in the backyard
- Ⓒ on the porch steps
- Ⓓ at the kitchen table

6 Which word best describes Elizabeth's father?

- Ⓐ helpful
- Ⓑ happy
- Ⓒ unfriendly
- Ⓓ distracted

7 How would you describe Elizabeth? Include two examples that show what type of person she is.

_____

_____

_____

_____

_____

_____

_____

_____

_____

_____

_____

_____

_____

_____

_____

_____

_____

Skill 6: Recognize Cause and Effect

Cause and effect questions ask about events that are connected to each other in some way.

CAUSE   the event that leads to the effect—*The wind is blowing hard.*
EFFECT   the result of the event—*The tree falls down.*

Directions: Read the passage below. The passage is followed by questions that can be answered by recognizing cause and effect. Use this passage to answer all the questions on pages 27–29.

Rainforests

Tropical rainforests are very dense, warm, and wet areas that are home to millions of animals and plants. The major rainforests, all of which are located near the equator, are in South America, Africa, and southeast Asia. The largest of these is the Amazon rainforest in South America. These ecosystems have existed for millions of years. They are vitally important to Earth's ecology.

As the name suggests, rainforests get a great deal of rain. In fact, it is almost always raining in these tropical forests. Because of the wet conditions, these areas rarely have forest fires. Rainforests get at least eighty inches of rain a year, and some may get as much as four hundred inches. One reason rainforests get so much precipitation is because they have a steady temperature, which is usually between 75 and 80 degrees Fahrenheit. This unique environment allows rainforests to recycle and clean water. Water evaporates from the oceans, clouds form, and rain falls on the rainforest. Later, the forest plants release moisture back into the atmosphere, and this water evaporates back into the air. When rainforests are destroyed, less moisture is released into the atmosphere, fewer clouds form, and there is a decline in rainfall.

More species live in rainforests than in any other parts of the world. This is probably due to the good living conditions: the weather is always warm, and water is always available. Rainforests teem with life from the forest floor all the way up to the tops of the tallest trees, which may be 100 feet high. Down below, bugs of all kinds scurry among the plants, jaguars hunt their prey, and alligators lurk in swamps. Above them, monkeys swing from tree to tree, parrots perch on branches, and tiny hummingbirds search for nectar.

Many people live in the rainforests. Some tribes have lived for thousands of years in small villages scattered throughout the rainforests. Their clothing and food come from the resources they find there. They hunt and fish. They gather plants and fruit to eat. But their way of life is threatened, and their numbers are declining. The main reason for this is disease. Having lived in isolation for so long, the people of the rainforest do not have resistance to many of the infections brought in from the outside world. Another reason is that the rainforests are getting smaller. When land is cleared for settlements and trees are cut down for lumber, it causes the people who live there to be displaced from their homes.

Indian hut on river bank, Brazil, circa 1900.
Photo courtesy of the Library of Congress.

Much harm has come to rainforests in recent years. The destruction is due to agricultural expansion, logging, oil exploration, and mining. This devastation is hurting the balance of nature on Earth. When large trees are forested for lumber and paper, the result is fewer trees and, therefore, less absorption of carbon dioxide. Increased levels of carbon dioxide in the air cause Earth's temperature to rise. Such an increase in temperature can cause flooding and climate disturbances like El Niño.

Taking away the environment in which many species of animals live can have a devastating effect as well. For example, the Brazil Nut tree cannot reproduce without a certain type of bee that pollinates its flowers. It also needs a certain type of rainforest rodent to open its seeds. If either of these animals becomes extinct, the Brazilian nut probably would too. This cause-and-effect relationship goes on and on, affecting all of us who inhabit this planet.

Modeled Instruction

Directions: Below is an example of a question that can be answered by recognizing cause and effect. Follow the strategy that is explained to help choose the correct answer.

---

1 What is one effect of the moist conditions in the rainforests?

Ⓐ Many tribes live in the rainforests.

Ⓑ Trees are cut down for lumber.

Ⓒ There are rarely any forest fires.

Ⓓ The rainforests are being destroyed.

Strategy: Look for key words in the question to help you figure out where to look in the passage for your answer. If the question gives you the cause, then you must find the effect or what happens. If the question gives you the effect, then you must find the cause.

Use this strategy to decide which answer is correct.

 Ⓐ Many tribes live in the rainforests.

Paragraph four discusses the people who live in the rainforests. It does not mention the wet climate in this paragraph. Nowhere in the passage is the wet climate given as a reason for people living in the rainforest. Therefore, *choice "A" cannot be correct.*

 Ⓒ There are rarely any forest fires.

The second paragraph states that it is almost always raining in the rainforest. Because of the wet conditions forest fires are rare. Therefore, *choice "C" is the correct answer.*

 Ⓑ Trees are cut down for lumber.

In the fourth and fifth paragraphs, cutting down trees is given as one of the causes of the destruction of rainforests. But it does not state here, or anywhere else in the passage, that the climate is the reason that trees are being cut down. Therefore, *choice "B" cannot be correct.*

 Ⓓ The rainforests are being destroyed.

The passage mentions in paragraphs four and five that the rainforests are being destroyed, but nothing indicates that this destruction is the result of the wet climate. Therefore, *choice "D" cannot be correct.*

Directions: Use the hints provided to answer the questions below. For question 2, you must choose the correct answer. For question 3, you will need to write out your answer.

---

2 **What happens when there is too much carbon dioxide in the air?**

Ⓐ Plants release more moisture.

Ⓑ The rain is cleaned.

Ⓒ The Brazil Nut Tree dies.

Ⓓ Earth's temperature rises.

Hint: Too much carbon dioxide in the air is the cause of something. Look through the passage to find what the effect is. Look for the key words "carbon dioxide" to help you find the part of the passage where this information can be found.

---

3 **What causes the decline in population of people who live in the rainforest?**

_____

_____

_____

_____

_____

_____

_____

_____

_____

_____

_____

_____

_____

_____

_____

_____

_____

Hint: Look through the passage to find details about the people of the rainforest that explain the causes of their decline.

Independent Study

Directions: Answer the following questions on your own. For questions 4, 5, and 6, choose the correct answer. For question 7, you must write out your answer.

---

4 **What happens when Earth's temperature rises?**

Ⓐ The tribes move out of the forest.

Ⓑ The Brazil Nut becomes extinct.

Ⓒ There are fewer fires in the rainforests.

Ⓓ There are floods and climate disturbances.

---

5 **Which of the following is NOT a reason for protecting the rainforests?**

Ⓐ Rainforests are a beautiful part of nature.

Ⓑ Rainforests help maintain Earth's balance.

Ⓒ Rainforests are home to many plants and animals.

Ⓓ Rainforests are a good place to build new communities.

---

6 **As discussed in the passage, if a certain type of bee becomes extinct—**

Ⓐ we would not have any honey to eat

Ⓑ rainforest flowers would be pollinated

Ⓒ the Brazil Nut could become extinct

Ⓓ a rainforest rodent would become extinct

---

7 **What causes the destruction of rainforests? Explain at least two causes that are discussed in the passage.**

_____

_____

_____

_____

_____

_____

_____

_____

_____

_____

_____

_____

_____

_____

_____

_____

Skill 7: Compare and Contrast

To compare means that you must tell how things are alike. To contrast means that you must tell how things are different. Compare and contrast questions may ask you to compare or contrast people, things, places, or events.

Directions: Read the passage below. The passage is followed by questions that can be answered by comparing or contrasting. Use this passage to answer all the questions on pages 31–33.

Bookworms Meet

Jeff loved to read and had decided to form a book club to share his interest with others his age. Five classmates attended the first meeting of the book club, and they all discussed what kinds of books they liked to read. Some preferred historical fiction while other readers liked adventure, and one individual favored science fiction. In order to choose a book that they would all enjoy reading, the group decided that each member should come to the next meeting with four book ideas. Then, they would meet the following week to make a selection from those choices.

So that Saturday, Jeff went to the library to look for books that interested him. After looking through the shelves, he made a list of four possible books, and wrote down information about each one.

Miss Ellen by Lisa Sanders
Length: 176 pages
Written in: 1971
Summary: Lori and Dan, life-long neighbors who are in high school, both hope to become writers. One way they hone their skills is by writing sarcastic descriptions of people with whom they have brief encounters: a clerk in a store, a bus driver, someone they pass on the street. But when one of these people suddenly enters their lives, Lori and Dan begin to appreciate the complexity of each individual.

A Committee of One by Dana Deane
Length: 272 pages
Written in: 1990s
Summary: Jeremy refuses to contribute his time to a high school fundraiser, because it's for a cause he cannot support. The pressure grows as friends, family, and even faculty members urge him to join them in their efforts. Then encouragement comes from a surprising source, someone he never thought of as a potential friend.

Just Yesterday by Elton Clay
Length: 188 pages
Written in: 1998
Summary:
This is a story about Jabar, a teenage boy whose classmate has died in a car accident. Until this loss, he has seen the world as divided into two groups—his friends and the others. But, when one of "the others" reaches out to him, he discovers that grief is universal and sharing the pain does help.

Tell Me Now by Carole DeMarro

Length: 176 pages

Written in: 1973

Summary: Mr. Major, the new science teacher, is pleasant, but many students don't find him particularly interesting. But Mr. Major understands people. As he gets to know his classes, he observes and he listens to what is not said, as well as what is said. He gradually becomes aware of one student's hidden pain and helps her find a solution that eases the burden.

When it was time for the club members to select a book to read, Jeff was pleased when one of his was picked. The unanimous choice was *Tell Me Now*. It reminded everyone of Mrs. Dalton, a popular teacher in the school, who also had a reputation for being a good listener, and they always wondered what she knew about students' lives. They congratulated Jeff for his book selection and for starting the book club. Things were off to a great start.

Modeled Instruction

Directions: Below is an example of a question that can be answered by comparing and contrasting information in the passage. Follow the strategy that is explained to help choose the correct answer.

---

1   What one thing do all the books have in common?

Ⓐ They are all about teenagers.

Ⓑ They all take place in Texas.

Ⓒ They are all under 300 pages long.

Ⓓ They all have male main characters.

Strategy: Making lists can help you to compare and contrast. You can make one list that tells how things are alike and another to tell how they are different. These lists can be used to help answer questions that ask you to compare and contrast.

Use this strategy to decide which answer is correct.

 Ⓐ They are all about teenagers.

The book *Tell Me Now* is about a science teacher, while the other books are about teenagers. Because one book is about a grown man, *choice "A" cannot be correct*.

 Ⓒ They are all under 300 pages long.

The length of each book is listed. The longest book is *A Committee of One*, which is 272 pages long. Therefore, *choice "C" must be the correct answer*.

 Ⓑ They all take place in Texas.

The notes tell when each book was written, but not where they take place. Because we do not know where the stories take place, *choice "B" cannot be correct*.

Ⓓ They all have male main characters.

Miss Ellen is a story about Lori and Dan, a boy and girl in high school. Because one of the main characters is female, *choice "D" cannot be correct*.

Guided Instruction

Directions: Use the hints provided to answer the questions below. For question 2, you must choose the correct answer. For question 3, you will need to write out your answer.

---

2 **What is one way that *Miss Ellen* is similar to *Tell Me Now*?**

Ⓐ *Miss Ellen* is about a boy and a girl.

Ⓑ *Miss Ellen* has two main characters.

Ⓒ *Miss Ellen* has a female author.

Ⓓ *Miss Ellen* is 176 pages long.

Hint: All of the details listed are true, but only one tells how the two books are similar. Read the details about each book again. Which detail is true about both books, and which details are only true about *Miss Ellen?* You can make a Venn diagram to help you answer this question, or you can use the chart that you made for question 1.

Only in *Miss Ellen*   In both *Miss Ellen* and *Tell Me Now*   Only in *Tell Me Now*

---

3 **How are *A Committee of One* and *Tell Me Now* different?**

_____

_____

_____

_____

_____

_____

_____

_____

_____

_____

_____

_____

Hint: Read the information given about each book. Compare the dates written, lengths, and summaries. Tell how the two are different.

Independent Study

Directions: Answer the following questions on your own. For questions 4, 5, and 6, choose the correct answer. For question 7, you must write out your answer.

---

4 **Which books were both written during the same decade?**

Ⓐ *Miss Ellen* and *A Committee of One*

Ⓑ *Just Yesterday* and *Tell Me Now*

Ⓒ *Tell Me Now* and *A Committee of One*

Ⓓ *A Committee of One* and *Just Yesterday*

---

5 **Which of the following is true about three out of the four books?**

Ⓐ They are written before the year 1965.

Ⓑ They are stories about teachers.

Ⓒ They are stories about teenaged people.

Ⓓ They are about making dreams come true.

---

6 **How are *Just Yesterday* and *A Committee of One* alike?**

Ⓐ The main characters have to deal with a tragic loss.

Ⓑ The main characters see another person in a new way.

Ⓒ The books are written by the same author.

Ⓓ The books take place in the same town and state.

---

7 **In what ways do *Miss Ellen* and *A Committee of One* differ from each other?**

_____

_____

_____

_____

_____

_____

_____

_____

_____

_____

_____

_____

_____

_____

_____

A Skill 8: Distinguish Fact from Opinion

To answer some questions you must be able to identify which statements are facts and which are opinions. For example:

FACT   a statement that **is true**—*There are 50 states in the United States.*
OPINION   a statement that someone **believes is true**—*My state is the most beautiful.*

Directions: Read the passage below. The passage is followed by questions that can be answered by distinguishing fact from opinion. Use this passage to answer all the questions on pages 35–37.

Make a Difference

Dear Editor,

    I am writing to you about the horrible waste that goes on in our school every day. I am referring to Williamson High's lack of a school-wide recycling program. Every day I witness soda cans being tossed in the garbage. I see students writing on only one side of a piece of paper. I watch teachers make extra copies and then throw some, or even all of them, away. I even saw the trashcan in our science room filled to overflowing with newspapers. This is the same science room where just last month we studied the benefits of recycling.

    Perhaps our student body and faculty need a review lesson on what recycling is and why we should do it. To recycle means to find ways to convert garbage and trash into usable materials. Every American produces four pounds of trash a day. That means that at our school, a student body of 500 and a faculty of 100 produce about 10,000 pounds of trash a week. If we could recycle twenty-five percent of this trash, which is the national goal, we could reduce our weekly rubbish pile by 2,500 pounds. Such a reduction would not only save landfill space, but it would also conserve our nation's natural resources.

    Recycling at the school level is important for many reasons. First of all, because we are all individuals rather than a family unit, we are using extra packaging. For example, when a family buys soda, they may purchase one two-liter bottle to provide enough drinks for five people. However, when we are at school, each of those five people buys one twenty-ounce bottle of soda. This increases the plastic use by five times what we might use at home. Furthermore, the very nature of education is to study the printed word. Thus, paper use and consumption are at a very high volume. We print from our computers, and we take tests on copy paper. We take notes in our paper-filled notebooks. I am not saying we shouldn't use so much paper, but I am saying we should recycle paper whenever we can. (Of course, if teachers want to cut down on how many tests they give, I'm sure students would not object!)

    The benefits of recycling cannot be dismissed. Recycling saves energy and conserves our natural resources. Recycling reduces our need for larger landfills. And recycling decreases pollution and loss of trees. There is, in fact, no reason not to recycle. Any excuses that are offered indicate ignorance of the facts or an unwillingness to make an effort. But, there are no valid excuses, and the students of Williamson High need to demand that our school develop an effective recycling program. It wouldn't be difficult, and it would save money. Some people think that the little things they could do don't have an impact on the environment, but these people are wrong. Recycling just one glass bottle saves enough electricity to light a 100-watt bulb for four hours! The cumulative effects of recycling are obvious, too. If everyone in this country who reads a morning paper recycled it, almost 50,000 trees would be saved. Every ton of recycled paper that is used saves 10 gallons of water. Recycling matters.

It would not be difficult to implement a school-wide recycling program. If our cafeterias had recycling bins near the vending machines and garbage cans, all those soda cans and plastic bottles would be thrown in the bins instead of the trashcans. It is no more difficult to toss a can into one container than into another. Classrooms, the library, and administrative offices should have separate bins for recycled paper and newspapers. Using different colored bins would help distinguish them.

What we do, or do not do, in this school matters. We must positively affect the future of our world. Last year in our state alone recycling programs successfully recycled over 128,000 tons of paper, glass, metals, and plastic. That is an impressive number. Let's add to it, Williamson High! Rah-rah, give an "R" for "Recycle!"

Ellen Myers
Sophomore class

Modeled Instruction

Directions: Below is an example of a question that can be answered by distinguishing fact from opinion in the passage. Follow the strategy that is explained to help choose the correct answer.

1 **Which statement from the passage is a fact?**

Ⓐ That is an impressive number.

Ⓑ Every ton of recycled paper used saves 10 gallons of water.

Ⓒ The benefits of recycling cannot be dismissed.

Ⓓ It would not be difficult to implement a school-wide recycling program.

Strategy: To tell if a statement is a fact or an opinion, think about what you can prove. Statements that can be proven are facts. If a statement cannot be proven, it is an opinion. Use the information in the passage to help determine which statements are facts and which are opinions.

Use this strategy to decide which answer is correct.

Ⓐ **That is an impressive number.**

Although 128,000 tons is a large number, it is not necessarily impressive to everyone. Therefore, *choice "A" cannot be correct.*

Ⓒ **The benefits of recycling cannot be dismissed.**

Anyone can choose to dismiss, or reject, the benefits of recycling, and some people will. Since this statement cannot be proven, *choice "C" cannot be the correct answer.*

Ⓑ **Every ton of recycled paper used saves 10 gallons of water.**

If you were to figure out how much water it takes to make new paper, you could prove that using recycled paper saves water. Since you can prove this, it must be a fact. Therefore, *choice "B" must be the correct answer.*

Ⓓ **It would not be difficult to implement a school-wide recycling program.**

One person may think that having a recycling program would be easy, but another person might think it would be hard. Since you cannot prove that it would be easy, *choice "D" cannot be correct.*

Guided Instruction

Directions: Use the hints provided to answer the questions below. For question 2, you must choose the correct answer. For question 3, you will need to write out your answer.

2 **Which sentence from the passage is an opinion?**

Ⓐ "Recycling saves energy and natural resources."

Ⓑ "Every day, I witness soda cans being tossed in the garbage."

Ⓒ "It is no more difficult to toss a can into one container than into another."

Ⓓ "Every ton of recycled paper that is used saves ten gallons of water."

Hint: Read the answer choices one at a time. To find the statement that is an opinion, ask yourself which statement you cannot prove.

3 **Read the following sentence from the passage:**

"Every American produces four pounds of trash a day."

Is this statement an example of a fact or an opinion? Explain your answer.

Hint: Think about what makes a statement a fact or an opinion. Ask yourself if the statement tells about something that **is true** or something that someone **believes is true**.

Independent Study

Directions: Answer the following questions on your own. For questions 4, 5, and 6, choose the correct answer. For question 7, you must write out your answer.

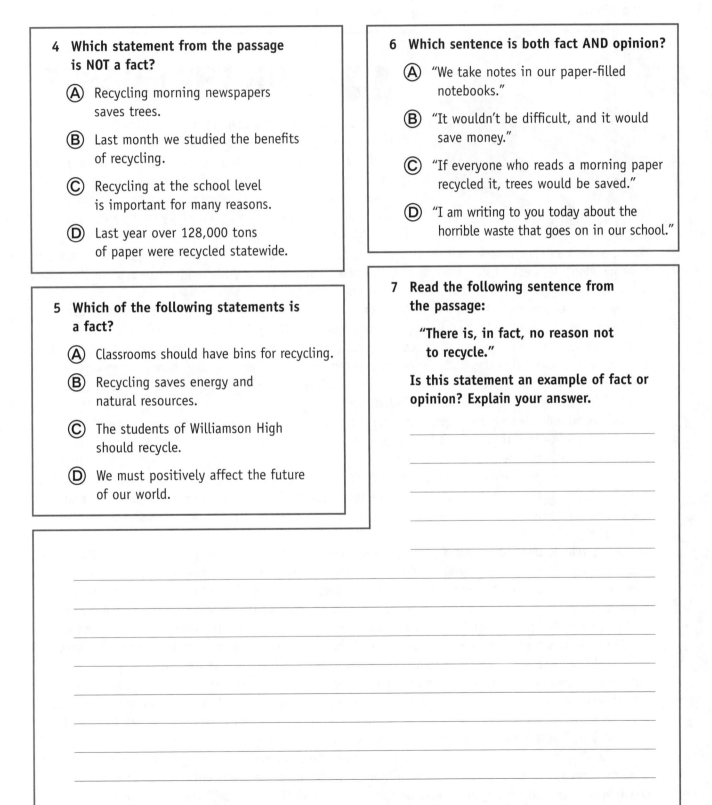

4 **Which statement from the passage is NOT a fact?**

Ⓐ Recycling morning newspapers saves trees.

Ⓑ Last month we studied the benefits of recycling.

Ⓒ Recycling at the school level is important for many reasons.

Ⓓ Last year over 128,000 tons of paper were recycled statewide.

5 **Which of the following statements is a fact?**

Ⓐ Classrooms should have bins for recycling.

Ⓑ Recycling saves energy and natural resources.

Ⓒ The students of Williamson High should recycle.

Ⓓ We must positively affect the future of our world.

6 **Which sentence is both fact AND opinion?**

Ⓐ "We take notes in our paper-filled notebooks."

Ⓑ "It wouldn't be difficult, and it would save money."

Ⓒ "If everyone who reads a morning paper recycled it, trees would be saved."

Ⓓ "I am writing to you today about the horrible waste that goes on in our school."

7 **Read the following sentence from the passage:**

"There is, in fact, no reason not to recycle."

Is this statement an example of fact or opinion? Explain your answer.

_____

_____

_____

_____

_____

_____

_____

_____

_____

_____

_____

Skill 9: Predict Outcomes

To predict an outcome means you try to figure out what will happen next or in the future. The answers are not stated in the passage. However, details from the passage can help you to predict outcomes.

Directions: Read the passage below. The passage is followed by questions that can be answered by predicting outcomes. Use this passage to answer all the questions on pages 39–41.

A DAY ON THE COURTS

Today the volleyball team of Andover High School would be competing in an all-day tournament. Rachel, Stephanie, and Cecilia could hardly wait, and Coach Vellone was eager for the opportunity, too. Coach Vellone had advised the girls to pack some snacks to munch on throughout the day. "Your appetite will show up between games," Coach Vellone warned the team.

Rachel and Stephanie each packed a cooler, including juice boxes, peanut butter crackers, fruit, and even some candy. Cecilia, having forgotten to pack her snack the previous night, hurriedly tossed a bottle of water and a banana in her duffel bag as she ran out the door. She'd eaten a bigger breakfast than usual, and couldn't imagine being very hungry later.

The team assembled in the school parking lot early in the morning, Coach Vellone took attendance, and then they all boarded the bus. During the hour-long ride, the girls chatted excitedly about the challenge ahead, sang songs, and reviewed their game strategy. As they approached the building where the tournament was being staged, they were impressed by its immensity. A huge banner hanging over the entrance announced, "Avon Sports Arena: Saturday, September 3rd, Welcome Girls Volleyball Teams; Sunday, September 4th, Welcome All-Star Indoor Soccer Players."

The squad unloaded all their equipment and personal belongings, but as they walked away from the bus, Stephanie realized that she had left her sweatshirt behind. She reassured herself with the thought that it would probably be hot in the building. Once inside, the group quickly staked out a corner to camp in for the day and proceeded to warm up. As they ran laps around the arena and then performed stretching exercises, other teams were doing the same. One team, called the Falcons, had a portable stereo that filled the gymnasium air with upbeat music, while also serving to energize the Falcons. "I wish we had thought of that!" Rachel lamented.

Coach Vellone unpacked some of the equipment while the players did exercises to warm up their cold muscles. Rummaging through the entire duffel bag, she searched in vain for her clipboard. "Don't tell me I forgot it!" she muttered to herself. Finally, exasperated, she conceded that she had and gave herself a silent scolding. After the girls had sufficiently limbered up, they began their drills with Rachel serving to the team while the other girls practiced receiving until it was time for the competition to commence.

After the girls played and were victorious in their first game, Coach Vellone informed them that they were not scheduled to compete again for another two hours. "Eat some of your snacks to keep up your energy, but don't eat them all. You'll need some after our next game, too." Rachel munched on her crackers and gulped down her juice while Cecilia nibbled at her banana. Stephanie noticed that Cecilia hadn't packed very much to satisfy her hunger for the long day. "Aren't you going to be hungry later?" she asked her friend.

"Probably," agreed Cecilia, regretting the mistake she had made.

While they had been playing, the arena had seemed hot. But now that the girls were just sitting and analyzing the other teams' play, the air conditioning made the air feel very chilly. Stephanie shivered until Coach Vellone loaned her an extra sweatshirt she had packed. "Here you go," the coach tossed the sweatshirt to Stephanie. "I don't suppose you packed a clipboard instead of a sweatshirt, did you, Steph?"

"Sorry," Stephanie shook her head, snuggling gratefully into the heavy sweatshirt.

By the day's end, the Andover team had been triumphant in three games and defeated in one. During the play Coach Vellone scribbled notes about the skills they needed to improve. Her handwriting was messy and almost illegible because her paper had bent and ripped as she jotted down her ideas. Her knee was definitely not a good substitute for her clipboard. "I hope I'll be able to read these on Monday," she grumbled.

The bus ride home was more subdued than the morning's bus ride. Each team member was physically exhausted, but emotionally elated by a job well done. After Cecilia fell asleep, her growling stomach made her friends laugh and wish they had a tape recorder, so they could tease her later.

When they arrived back at the school parking lot, each team member thanked Coach Vellone for the great day. "Practice is at three o'clock sharp on Monday!" she reminded them. "Don't forget your clipboard!" the girls teased as they dispersed to the cars where their parents were waiting to welcome them home.

Modeled Instruction

Directions: Below is an example of a question that can be answered by using information from the passage to predict an outcome. Follow the strategy that is explained to help choose the correct answer.

---

1 What will probably occur at the arena the day after the volleyball tournament?

Ⓐ There will be a volleyball practice.

Ⓑ The arena will be closed for Sunday.

Ⓒ There will be an indoor soccer tournament.

Ⓓ There will be another volleyball tournament.

Strategy: Do not look for the answer in the passage. Instead look for details that will help you to make a prediction. Try to find details in the passage that are related in some way to the question. Ask yourself what these details suggest.

Use this strategy to decide which answer is correct.

Ⓐ **There will be a volleyball practice.**

The details in the passage show that the girls traveled from their school to the arena. Also, the details show that when the team returns to the school parking lot, the coach reminds them to be at practice on Monday. Since it does not make sense that the team would travel to practice everyday, *choice "A" is not correct.*

Ⓒ **There will be an indoor soccer tournament.**

Details in the passage note that the sign on the building welcomes indoor soccer players the day after it welcomes the volleyball players. Because the sign welcomes the two groups the same way, it suggests that they are there for similar reasons. Therefore, *choice "C" must be the correct answer.*

Ⓑ **The arena will be closed for Sunday.**

It would be possible that a sports arena be closed on a Sunday. However, the arena sign suggests that they are holding an event that Sunday. There, it does not make sense that the arena would be closed. *Choice "B" is not the correct choice.*

Ⓓ **There will be another volleyball tournament.**

Details in the passage show that the volleyball tournament is only for one day. Therefore, *choice "D" cannot be the correct choice.*

Guided Instruction

Directions: Use the hints provided to answer the questions below. For question 2, you must choose the correct answer. For question 3, you will need to write out your answer.

2 The next time the volleyball team travels to a tournament—

Ⓐ Cecilia will probably pack a bigger snack

Ⓑ Stephanie will keep her sweatshirt on

Ⓒ Coach Vellone will pack snacks for the team

Ⓓ Coach Vellone will not bring an extra sweatshirt

Hint: Look for details in the passage that suggest something each person would do differently next time. Do any of them do or say something to suggest what they might do differently?

3 What does Rachel want to bring with them the next time the team goes to a tournament?

_____

_____

_____

_____

_____

_____

_____

_____

_____

_____

_____

_____

_____

_____

_____

_____

Hint: Read the parts of the passage that mention Rachel. Think about what she does and what she says. Use these details to help you predict what she will take to the next tournament.

Independent Study

Directions: Answer the following questions on your own. For questions 4, 5, and 6, choose the correct answer. For question 7, you must write out your answer.

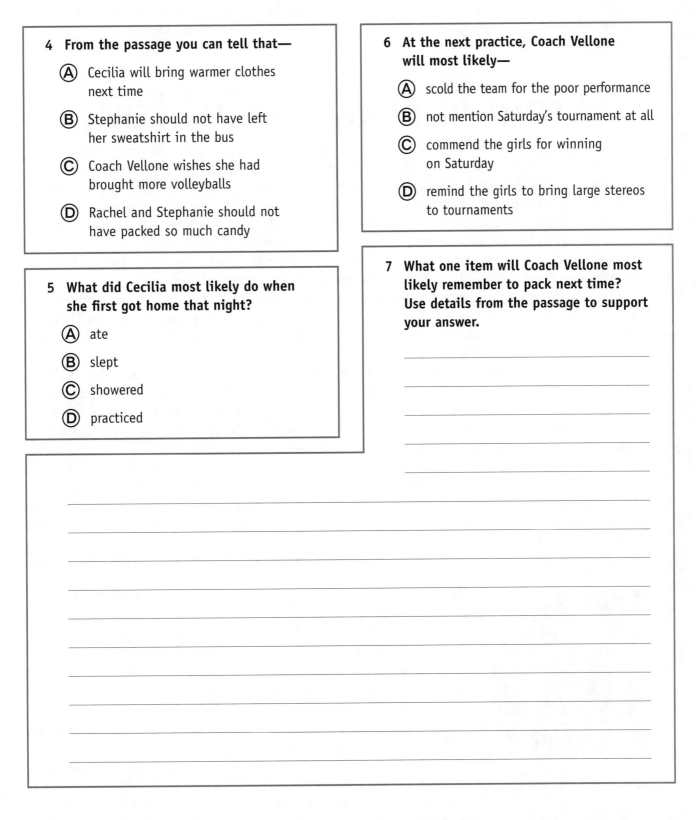

4 **From the passage you can tell that—**

Ⓐ Cecilia will bring warmer clothes next time

Ⓑ Stephanie should not have left her sweatshirt in the bus

Ⓒ Coach Vellone wishes she had brought more volleyballs

Ⓓ Rachel and Stephanie should not have packed so much candy

5 **What did Cecilia most likely do when she first got home that night?**

Ⓐ ate

Ⓑ slept

Ⓒ showered

Ⓓ practiced

6 **At the next practice, Coach Vellone will most likely—**

Ⓐ scold the team for the poor performance

Ⓑ not mention Saturday's tournament at all

Ⓒ commend the girls for winning on Saturday

Ⓓ remind the girls to bring large stereos to tournaments

7 **What one item will Coach Vellone most likely remember to pack next time? Use details from the passage to support your answer.**

_____

_____

_____

_____

_____

_____

_____

_____

_____

_____

_____

_____

Skill 10: Draw Conclusions

To draw conclusions you must use the information in the passage plus your own judgment. To answer questions that require you to draw conclusions you must think about what the information in the passage suggests. Conclusions must be based on facts found in the passage.

Directions: Read the passage below. The passage is followed by questions that can be answered by drawing conclusions. Use this passage to answer all the questions on pages 43–45.

From Tomboy to First Lady

Elizabeth Virginia Wallace, born on February 13, 1885, was the oldest of five children. She grew up in Independence, Missouri where her father was the son of the town's mayor and her mother was the daughter of a wealthy businessman. Bess, who was nicknamed after her mother's college roommate, was a tomboy who enjoyed sports during an era when girls were expected to excel at sewing and cooking. She was a strong tennis player, loved riding horses, and played baseball. One story tells of Bess when she was thirteen years old. On her way to dance class, she was dressed in a ruffled party dress and shiny new patent leather shoes. But she never made it to class. Instead she was sidetracked by her brother, Frank, who asked her to pinch hit for his baseball team. Bess hit a grand slam and won the game.

Little did that young girl know that she would one day become the wife of an American president. Bess and Harry Truman first met at a church function when they were just five and six years old. Harry admired the "blue-eyed blonde haired princess" he met that day, but Bess thought him a scrawny, bookish boy with whom she had nothing in common.

Her father, to whom Bess was very attached, was a good father but a poor businessman. In 1903, upset about his financial failures, he committed suicide. This event changed the lives of Bess, her mother, and her brothers who were forced to leave their home and move in with her mother's parents. Bess tried to help her grieving mother and watched over her younger brothers. The gossip that followed her father's untimely death disturbed Bess and was a factor in making her a very private person.

When Bess met Harry Truman again in 1910, she was more impressed than she had been at their first encounter. They began to exchange letters and see each other on a regular basis despite the disapproval of Mrs. Wallace who doubted that Truman would ever be a success in life. Nine long years later, when Harry returned from World War One, the two were married. When his business failed and Harry began his political career, Bess provided support and advice. They had a daughter in 1924 and named her Margaret. During all this time, they were living with Mrs. Wallace, a situation that cannot have been entirely comfortable given her view of Truman.

President Truman with First Lady Bess Truman at the airport in Washington just prior to the President's departure for Chicago to attend the Democratic National Convention, 1952. Photo courtesy of the Library of Congress.

When President Franklin D. Roosevelt died in office on April 12, 1945, Vice President Harry S. Truman was sworn in as the 33rd president of the United States of America. Bess Truman became the First Lady. Many people consider her one of the strongest first ladies in history. While at the White House, Bess did the bookkeeping, supervised all the money spent there, and worked for many charities. She acted as a personal adviser to her husband while he served his presidency, and she even helped write his speeches. Bess Truman had no college education, but she was an intelligent and knowledgeable woman who made noteworthy contributions to her country.

Bess Truman's style as First Lady differed from those that had preceded her. For example, she cancelled the weekly press conferences that Eleanor Roosevelt had held and instead gave weekly teas for the newswomen. Also, Bess disliked being photographed, and her feelings on the matter solidified after an unsettling experience she had when christening a military hospital plane. Despite her repeated attempts, the champagne bottle would not break. In the photos of the event that were published in the newspapers, Bess looked embarrassed and foolish. She was rarely photographed after this incident. Bess had other negative experiences with the public. At that time, some people believed Bess should end her involvement with the Daughters of the American Revolution because they had not allowed an African-American pianist to play at one of their events. Bess criticized the group's decision, but did not sever her connection with them. The controversy this caused made Bess remove herself further from the public eye.

When his term as president was over in 1953, Harry and Bess Truman left Washington, D.C. and returned to Independence, Missouri. They lived in the same house where Bess had spent most of the years before her marriage. After her husband's death in 1972, Bess continued to live in the house until she died in 1982 at the age of ninety-seven. In her will she left their home to the country. It is now a historic landmark.

Modeled Instruction

Directions: Below is an example of a question that can be answered by drawing conclusions about the passage. Follow the strategy that is explained to help choose the correct answer.

1 **Why do you think Bess Truman was considered a tomboy?**

Ⓐ because she liked to dance

Ⓑ because Frank nicknamed her that

Ⓒ because she enjoyed sports

Ⓓ because she liked a boy named Tom

Strategy: Look for details in the passage that help you to draw conclusions. Think about what these details tell you. Ask yourself what you can conclude from the facts you are given

Use this strategy to decide which answer is correct.

Ⓐ **because she liked to dance**

The passage does mention that Bess takes dance class. However, dance lessons are not an event reserved mostly for boys. Therefore, you cannot conclude that that is the reason Bess is called a tomboy. *Choice "A" cannot be the correct choice.*

Ⓒ **because she enjoyed sports**

The passage explains that girls did not usually play sports during that time. The term "tomboy" referred to girls who participated in what were considered "boys' activities." Bess acts like a boy by playing sports and is, therefore, referred to as a tomboy. From this you can conclude that *choice "C" must be the correct answer.*

Ⓑ **because Frank nicknamed her that**

There is no information that her brother considered Bess a tomboy. Therefore, *choice "B" cannot be the correct choice.*

Ⓓ **because she liked a boy named Tom**

No boy named Tom is mentioned anywhere in the passage. Therefore, *choice "D" cannot be correct.*

Guided Instruction

Directions: Use the hints provided to answer the questions below. For question 2, you must choose the correct answer. For question 3, you will need to write out your answer.

2 **You can conclude her father's death was devastating for Bess because—**

Ⓐ he was a financial failure who was unable to support his family

Ⓑ her family didn't have much money and that embarrassed her

Ⓒ people gossiped about him and the family's circumstances changed

Ⓓ she had to quit school and go to work to help her mother pay off the debts

Hint: Find details in the passage that tell about Bess and her father. Look for facts about the kind of relationship that they had. Ask yourself what you can conclude from this information.

3 **Why did many people consider Bess to be one of the strongest first ladies in America?**

_____

_____

_____

_____

_____

_____

_____

_____

_____

_____

_____

_____

_____

_____

_____

_____

Hint: Think about what Bess Truman did while her husband was in office. Ask yourself if the things she did showed strength. Think about what you can conclude from this information.

Independent Study

Directions: Answer the following questions on your own. For questions 4, 5, and 6, choose the correct answer. For question 7, you must write out your answer.

4 From the passage it can be concluded that Bess and her family moved in with her mother's family because—

Ⓐ they had no money

Ⓑ their house was old

Ⓒ they needed more room

Ⓓ their family was growing

5 Why did the Trumans move back to Independence, Missouri?

Ⓐ World War Two had begun.

Ⓑ Harry's presidential term was completed.

Ⓒ Bess wanted to leave the nation's capital.

Ⓓ They were asked to leave Washington, D.C.

6 How did Bess feel about Harry Truman when they first met?

Ⓐ excited

Ⓑ annoyed

Ⓒ fascinated

Ⓓ uninterested

7 How do you think Bess felt about a woman playing a part in her husband's career and finances?

_____

_____

_____

_____

_____

_____

_____

_____

_____

_____

_____

_____

_____

_____

_____

Skill 11: Make Inferences

To answer some questions you must make inferences. An inference is a decision or an opinion that is based upon information that is assumed. It is made from context or visual aids, such as maps or photos. Inferences are not based upon stated facts and are not always correct.

| INFORMATION | *Ann is ill.* |
| INFERENCE | *She will not go to school tomorrow.* |

Directions: Read the passage below. The passage is followed by questions that can be answered by making inferences. Use this passage to answer all the questions on pages 47–49.

A Day to Remember

Dear Diary,

I can't believe today was my first day of high school. I didn't get any sleep last night, because I was tossing and turning, worrying about today. On the bus ride this morning, Mia and I just sat silently staring out the windows instead of chatting and waving at the passing cars.

When I arrived this morning and tried to make my way to my locker, I couldn't believe how many people were crammed into the halls. For a while I thought that a lot of them were grown-ups, but then I realized they were seniors. Will I ever look that old? After I dumped my jacket in the locker, I headed off to my first class, very anxious about getting lost in this huge building, which I did in a way, but it turned out fine.

This was my schedule today. My first period is English with Mrs. Landry. She seems pleasant and I really enjoy English, so I don't anticipate any major problems in that class. The only difficulty is that I'm not a morning person, so on a scale from one to ten my alertness probably registers about one at that time of day. In second period computer lab, I was impressed by the up-to-date technology, and anticipate sharpening my skills in using graphics programs. Next is Home Economics and then gym, so my mornings are relatively stress-free. At lunch I sat with Maddie, Sam, and two boys I hadn't met before, and we all had a great time comparing our morning experiences. Maddie and Sam had been away all summer, so it was great to see them. After lunch I went upstairs for biology, and Mr. King seems nice, but very serious. What I dread most is the possibility that we'll have to dissect a frog, but some sophomores told me that every class has to do that. Sixth period is study hall, and I had so many assignments that I actually studied instead of socializing. And last, but not least, I have Algebra with Ms. Thomas who seems very strict, speaks too quickly, and makes the chalk screech when she writes incomprehensible problems on the board. We have twenty problems to do for homework, and I'd much prefer to read twenty books!

The high school building is such a huge place that I'm impressed with myself for getting lost only once. Well, not really lost, but confused. The Home Economics class meets in "Room 111-Kitchen," and I finally had to ask someone where Room 111-Kitchen was. This map of the right wing of the first floor shows why I had a problem finding it.

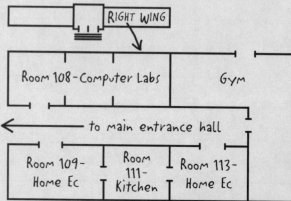

Between racing to classes on the first and second floors and stopping at my locker, I got too much exercise today! From now on I'll avoid sprinting up and down stairs all day and fighting the crowds, by carrying most of my books with me. So instead of training for track team, I'll do lots of weight lifting.

I do miss junior high school, though, because everything was so familiar and it was very gratifying to be the oldest students in the school. I miss knowing the teachers, too. I felt comfortable in most of my classes because I knew what each teacher expected from me. I wonder if I'll ever feel that way again.

Now, I better get going on those math problems. Only 20 more to go...

Donna, a high school student (WOW!)

Modeled Instruction

Directions: Below is an example of a question that can be answered by making inferences about the passage. Follow the strategy that is explained to help choose the correct answer.

> 1 **The high school is different from the school Donna attended last year because—**
>
> Ⓐ there are more students
>
> Ⓑ classes are more difficult
>
> Ⓒ everyone is less friendly
>
> Ⓓ the seniors look young

Strategy: Think about what the details in the diary entry suggest. You will not be able to find specific facts that tell you the answer. You must look at each answer and try to find details to support it. Ask yourself which answer makes the most sense.

Use this strategy to decide which answer is correct.

Ⓐ **there are more students**

Nowhere in the passage does it actually say that there are more students in the school, but details suggest this. Donna states that the students were crammed into the hallways and she had to fight the crowds, so you can infer that there are many students in the school. Therefore, *choice "A" would be the best answer.*

Ⓑ **classes are more difficult**

Donna discusses her class schedule, and describes some classes as easy and some as difficult. None of the details in the passage lead to a conclusion either way. Therefore, *choice "B" cannot be the correct answer.*

Ⓒ **everyone is less friendly**

Donna describes some of her teachers as nice, and when she has lunch with her friends Maddie and Sam she meets two new people. Also, she talks to some sophomores about the biology class. From this you can infer that the people at the school are friendly. Therefore, *choice "C" cannot be the correct choice.*

Ⓓ **the seniors look young**

The second paragraph says that the seniors look like teachers. Since the teachers are usually older, not younger, you cannot come to this conclusion. Therefore, *choice "D" cannot be correct.*

Guided Instruction

Directions: Use the hints provided to answer the questions below. For question 2, you must choose the correct answer. For question 3, you will need to write out your answer.

2 **Which of the following describes how Donna probably feels about going to high school?**

Ⓐ She wishes she were a high school senior.

Ⓑ She is excited and proud to be in high school.

Ⓒ She is afraid and anxious about being in high school.

Ⓓ She likes high school, but not as much as her old school.

Hint: Think about how Donna describes her first day of high school. Notice the details she includes, and even how she signs the entry. What can you infer from this information?

3 **Why did Donna have trouble finding Room 111-Kitchen?**

_____

_____

_____

_____

_____

_____

_____

_____

_____

_____

_____

_____

_____

_____

_____

_____

_____

_____

_____

Hint: Look at the layout of the first floor. Imagine that you are in the hall and looking at the room numbers.

Independent Study

Directions: Answer the following questions on your own. For questions 4, 5, and 6, choose the correct answer. For question 7, you must write out your answer.

4 **From the diary entry you can tell—**

Ⓐ Biology class is on the first floor

Ⓑ Donna likes Sam, but not Maddie

Ⓒ English is Donna's favorite subject

Ⓓ Donna had trouble finding the gym

5 **Why do you think Donna didn't see Maddie and Sam over the summer?**

Ⓐ Maddie and Sam were angry with Donna and didn't call her.

Ⓑ Maddie and Sam were out of town most of the summer.

Ⓒ Maddie doesn't like Sam and didn't want to get together.

Ⓓ Donna babysat so often that she didn't have time to see anyone.

6 **What do you think Donna's biggest concern was on her first day of high school?**

Ⓐ getting lost

Ⓑ failing a class

Ⓒ being late to class

Ⓓ falling asleep in class

7 **Why do you think Donna would rather read twenty books than do math problems?**

_____

_____

_____

_____

_____

_____

_____

_____

_____

_____

_____

_____

_____

_____

_____

_____

Skill 12: Analyze Point of View and Purpose

To analyze a point of view or the purpose in a passage, you need to try to put yourself in the place of the author.

POINT OF VIEW	what the author believes about a topic
PURPOSE	why the author wrote the passage

Directions: Read the letter below. The letter is followed by questions that can be answered by analyzing the author's point of view and purpose. Use this letter to answer all the questions on pages 51–53.

Nobody Understands Me!

That would be a valid complaint for almost any bat, because they just might be the most misunderstood animals in the United States. Many people think of bats as bloodsucking flying rats that launch unprovoked attacks on people but, in actuality, bats are very beneficial. Bats save crops by eating the insects that could ruin them. In fact, bats eat an astounding number of insects. A single bat can consume up to one thousand insects in just one hour. That fact alone starts to put things into perspective. And how often has a bat ruined your barbecue? Probably not as many times as a swarm of bloodthirsty mosquitoes has sent you scurrying inside.

There are over 1,000 different types of bats in the world, representing almost one quarter of all the mammal species. Yes, they are mammals, not birds, but they are the only known mammals that fly. Almost forty percent of bat species are endangered, which means that they are in danger of extinction. Bats are found throughout the United States. The state of Florida has seventeen types of bats, but Texas has its own claims to fame when it comes to bats. Twenty million bats inhabit Bracken Cave near the city of San Antonio in Texas, making it the most populated bat cave in the world. In Austin, Texas the Congress Avenue Bridge houses 1.5 million free-tail bats. From March to November, throngs of tourists congregate to watch the amazing spectacle of swarms of bats pouring forth from the cave.

The Bat Conservation International (BTI) is also based in Austin, Texas. Dr. Merlin Tuttle, a mammal expert who had been fascinated with bats since the age of nine, started the organization in 1982. World-famous for the conservation of bats and a leader in educating people about bats, BTI also conducts research on the animal. By providing information on this fascinating mammal, the organization hopes to dispel many of the public's misconceptions.

One such misconception is that bats are blind. Although they cannot differentiate between colors, bats can see and, in fact, they see better than humans can, especially at night. Also, bats use echolocation, another way of "seeing." They send out high-pitched signals that bounce off objects. By listening to the echo, the bat can determine how far away an object is, its size, and the direction in which it is moving. With all this information, the tiniest insects flitting through complete darkness are easy prey for a bat.

Another myth is that all bats have rabies and this, too, is erroneous. Less than one percent of bats carry the rabies virus, and in the last thirty years only about twenty people have contracted rabies from bats. More people sustain injuries or are killed by bee stings and dog attacks than by bat bites! Yet another ludicrous tale about bats is that they get entangled in people's hair. This illogical fear may have come from the fact that when bats are swooping after mosquitoes or other insects, they sometimes fly close to people's faces.

Perhaps the biggest misconception about bats, which arises from all those vampire movies, is that they suck people's blood. No bats in the United States feed on warm-blooded animals. There are some vampire bat species in Mexico, South America, and Central America, but their favorite targets are animals such as birds and cattle. With their sharp teeth, these bats cut a small hole in a sleeping animal's skin. The animal usually does not even feel it, because a chemical in bats' saliva numbs the skin. Bats don't prey on people, so you don't have to have any more nightmares about vampire bats.

In fact, bats are the ones who should be petrified. Several types of animals prey on bats, including snakes, owls, and hawks. Humans are having a large impact on bat populations by killing them, destroying their habitats, and disturbing their hibernation. The last factor is a major reason for the declining bat population. If a bat is aroused during hibernation, it can use up to three weeks of its hibernation energy, and may not have enough energy left to survive the rest of the winter.

Try to obtain more information about bats, and much of your anxiety about them is likely to disappear. There are sources of information, including your local zoo, books at your library, and web sites. You may end up being so fascinated by them that you'll plan a trip to Texas!

Modeled Instruction

Directions: Below is an example of a question that can be answered by analyzing the author's point of view and purpose. Follow the strategy that is explained to help choose the correct answer.

---

1 **The author of this essay probably believes that—**

Ⓐ bats cannot hurt people

Ⓑ people watch too many movies

Ⓒ people should learn more about bats

Ⓓ there are no informative books about bats

Strategy: Think about the entire passage, not just a section of it. In order to understand an author's point of view or purpose you must consider all of the information that is given. If you only focus on a few details you may get the wrong idea about what the author believes or is trying to say.

U s e   t h i s   s t r a t e g y   t o   d e c i d e   w h i c h   a n s w e r   i s   c o r r e c t .

 Ⓐ **bats cannot hurt people**

The author does say that bats are not as dangerous as most people believe them to be. However, the author does not say that bats cannot hurt people. Therefore, *choice "A" cannot be correct.*

 Ⓒ **people should learn more about bats**

In the beginning of the essay, the author explains that many people misconceptions about bats. Later in the essay, the author talks about how there is more to learn about bats and suggests ways to get more information. This suggests that the author believes people should learn more about bats. Therefore, *choice "C" is the correct answer.*

 Ⓑ **people watch too many movies**

In part of the essay, the author does suggest that people probably get the wrong idea from movies. However, there is no information that states people watch too many movies. Therefore, *choice "B" cannot be correct.*

 Ⓓ **there are no informative books about bats**

The last paragraph of the essay tells the reader to go to the library to find books about bats. Nowhere does the author state that there are no good books about bats. Therefore, *choice "D" cannot be the correct answer.*

Guided Instruction

Directions: Use the hints provided to answer the questions below. For question 2, you must choose the correct answer. For question 3, you will need to write out your answer.

2   **With which of the following statements would the author of the essay most likely agree?**

Ⓐ Only hibernating bats will hurt people.

Ⓑ People should be afraid of bees and dogs.

Ⓒ The more you understand about bats, the less likely you are to fear them.

Ⓓ The less you know about something, the less reason you have to worry about it.

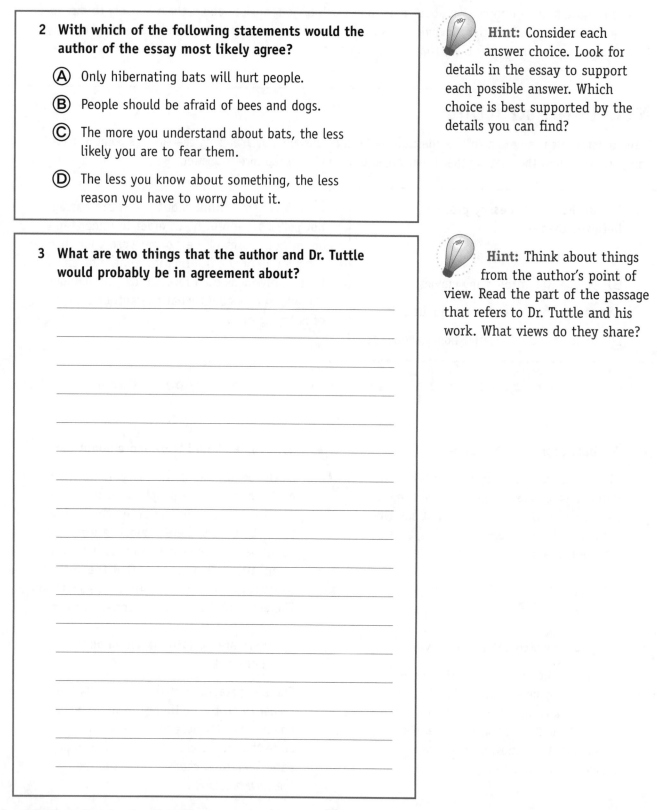

Hint: Consider each answer choice. Look for details in the essay to support each possible answer. Which choice is best supported by the details you can find?

3   **What are two things that the author and Dr. Tuttle would probably be in agreement about?**

_____

_____

_____

_____

_____

_____

_____

_____

_____

_____

_____

_____

_____

_____

_____

_____

_____

Hint: Think about things from the author's point of view. Read the part of the passage that refers to Dr. Tuttle and his work. What views do they share?

Independent Study

Directions: Answer the following questions on your own. For questions 4, 5, and 6, choose the correct answer. For question 7, you must write out your answer.

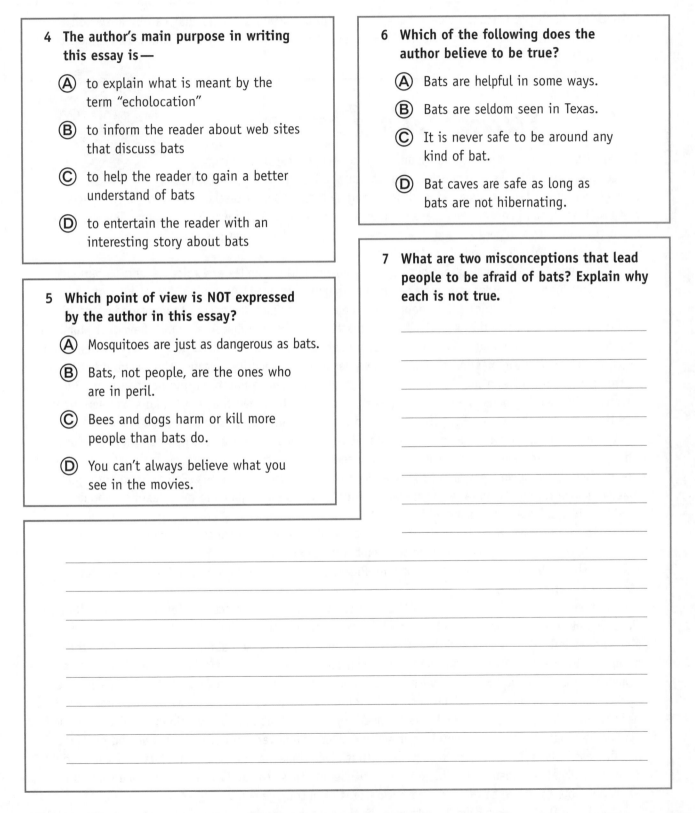

4 The author's main purpose in writing this essay is—

Ⓐ to explain what is meant by the term "echolocation"

Ⓑ to inform the reader about web sites that discuss bats

Ⓒ to help the reader to gain a better understand of bats

Ⓓ to entertain the reader with an interesting story about bats

5 Which point of view is NOT expressed by the author in this essay?

Ⓐ Mosquitoes are just as dangerous as bats.

Ⓑ Bats, not people, are the ones who are in peril.

Ⓒ Bees and dogs harm or kill more people than bats do.

Ⓓ You can't always believe what you see in the movies.

6 Which of the following does the author believe to be true?

Ⓐ Bats are helpful in some ways.

Ⓑ Bats are seldom seen in Texas.

Ⓒ It is never safe to be around any kind of bat.

Ⓓ Bat caves are safe as long as bats are not hibernating.

7 What are two misconceptions that lead people to be afraid of bats? Explain why each is not true.

_____

_____

_____

_____

_____

_____

_____

_____

_____

_____

_____

_____

_____

_____

_____

Skill 13: Identify Literary Forms and Sources of Information

To answer some questions you must be able to identify different types of passages. For example, you must know the difference between a poem and a story. Also, some questions will ask you to tell where you are likely to find different types of information. For example, information about current events might be found in a newspaper.

Directions: Read the passage below. The passage is followed by questions that can be answered by identifying literary forms and sources of information. Use this passage to answer all the questions on pages 55–57.

Juanita's Dream

Juanita loved writing poetry and aspired to be a poet. Almost unknowingly, she covered her notebooks with couplets and stanzas and lilting phrases that drifted through her mind as she daydreamed in class. During biology, while her teacher droned on about species of reptiles, Juanita had penned, "Your graceful greenness sweeps the sky," a wonderful opening line for a poem about the willow tree in her backyard. There were so many possible images she could use in this poem that she was certain it would be one of her favorites.

When Juanita told people about her literary ambitions, their smiles and raised eyebrows betrayed their views. Juanita's mother was more forthright, shaking her head and saying, "What kind of life is that? Most poets are not successful people, just dreamers. Pay more attention to your grades and less attention to the clouds in the sky." Her father's reaction was equally discouraging. "I have met plumbers, and doctors, and lawyers, but I have never met a poet! Is that really a job at all?" he asked. Her parents urged her to choose a profession that would give her financial security, because they wanted her to be a strong, independent woman. They suggested that she could write poetry during her free time. But Juanita witnessed her parents' long days of work, and had determined that most adults had very little free time. No, she thought to herself. She wanted to write poetry all the time.

Juanita tried to pretend that everyone's negative reactions did not affect her, but they did. For a while, she even stopped writing poetry. But the need to play with words overtook her again. It was while she was scribbling down ideas about the beauty of the crashing sea that Mrs. Perez, her eighth grade teacher, spoke to her. "Juanita, what are you doing?" she inquired, glancing over Juanita's shoulder.

"I, well, I..." Juanita stammered in response.

"Is that poetry you're writing?" Other students laughed as they heard the question.

"Yes," Juanita admittedly, red-faced with embarrassment.

"You should be studying your Shakespeare. Please return to that assignment," Mrs. Perez stated. "And see me after school."

At three o'clock Juanita returned to Mrs. Perez's room, ready to be scolded for not paying attention in class. Juanita was pleasantly surprised when Mrs. Perez told her she admired Juanita's appreciation of poetry and wanted to discuss poetry with her. That afternoon, they conversed about the beauty of poetry and its appeal to Juanita. After sharing one of her own poems with Juanita, Mrs. Perez asked Juanita to share some of her own writing. Simultaneously excited and nervous, Juanita showed her teacher a couple of poems that she considered to be her best, and eventually she shared her whole writing notebook. Mrs. Perez liked some of her poems, and didn't care as much for others. "But what I love about all of them," she had confided in Juanita, "is the joy you take in writing them. Whatever you do, continue writing poetry, but not in class," she said with a smile. "Anything that gives someone this much satisfaction must be right." Juanita received the positive feedback with gratitude and tucked it away in her mind. She wanted to always be able to return to these sympathetic words of encouragement.

Another gift Mrs. Perez gave Juanita were books containing information about different poetry styles and various poets' lives. Juanita's world expanded as she read volumes of poems from different eras and experimented with different styles. She inserted similes and metaphors into her writing to give it depth and sparkle. She consumed biographical volumes about poets, such as E. E. Cummings and William Carlos Williams. Juanita read poems by Emily Dickinson, a poet during the 1800s who lived the life of a recluse. She loved Dickinson's poem that begins, "Hope is the thing with feathers

> That perches in the soul,
> And sings the tune without the words,
> And never stops at all"

Learning about other poets' lives only fueled Juanita's desire to have a similar life for herself. One day as she gazed out the window at the willow tree, she suddenly realized the intensity of her commitment to her poetry. Smiling to herself, she envisioned the future time when another young poet would sit by a window reading *The Willow Tree and Other Poems* by Juanita Santros.

Modeled Instruction

Directions: Below is an example of a question that can be answered by identifying literary forms and sources of information. Follow the strategy that is explained to help choose the correct answer.

---

1 This passage is an example of—

(A) a story

(B) a poem

(C) an essay

(D) a biography

Strategy: Think about the following:

• What can you tell about the style in which the passage was written?

• What type of information can be found in the passage?

• Why might you choose to read the passage?

Asking yourself these three questions will help you to choose the correct answer.

Use this strategy to decide which answer is correct.

think

(A) a story

A story can tell about people and events. Some stories are true and some are made up. The purpose of a story is to entertain. All of these accurately describe the passage. Based on this information, *choice "A" is correct.*

think

(C) an essay

An essay is usually written about one topic or idea. It provides information that expresses the author's point of view. Since the main purpose of the passage is NOT to give information or express a point of view, *choice "C" cannot be the correct answer.*

think

(B) a poem

In poems, words are arranged in patterns. Sometimes words in poems rhyme and sometimes the words can be spoken in rhythm. There is a poem within the story, but the whole passage does not have the characteristics of a poem. Therefore, *choice "B" cannot be correct.*

think

(D) a biography

A biography tells about the life of a person. Usually biographies are about famous or well-known people. Although this passage is about Juanita, it does not tell about her entire life. Also, Juanita is a character in a story, not a real person. Therefore, *choice "D" cannot be the answer.*

Guided Instruction

Directions: Use the hints provided to answer the questions below. For question 2, you must choose the correct answer. For question 3, you will need to write out your answer.

---

2 The purpose of this passage is—

(A) to teach

(B) to inform

(C) to entertain

(D) to persuade

Hint: Describe the passage to yourself. Think about why the passage was probably written. Why might someone choose to read this passage?

---

3 Explain how you can tell that this passage is NOT an example of a myth.

_____

_____

_____

_____

_____

_____

_____

_____

_____

_____

_____

_____

_____

_____

_____

_____

_____

_____

_____

_____

Hint: A myth is a story about imaginary creatures, heroes, and gods. It is often used to explain the customs or beliefs of a group of people. Think about how this compares to the passage you read.

Independent Study

Directions: Answer the following questions on your own. For questions 4, 5, and 6, choose the correct answer. For question 7, you must write out your answer.

4 The poets' biographies that Juanita read were most likely written —

Ⓐ to persuade students to write poetry

Ⓑ to teach other poets the rules of poetry

Ⓒ to provide information about the poets' lives and work

Ⓓ to prove that their poems were amazing artistic works

6 Where would you most likely find this passage?

Ⓐ in a magazine for poetry writing

Ⓑ in the art section of a newspaper

Ⓒ in a book containing a collection of folk tales

Ⓓ in a book containing a collection of short stories

5 What should Juanita read if she wants to learn more about how to write poetry?

Ⓐ a myth about the first poem

Ⓑ a book about poetry techniques

Ⓒ a letter written by Emily Dickinson

Ⓓ a biography of William Carlos Williams

7 How would this passage be different if it were written as a play?

_____

_____

_____

_____

_____

_____

_____

_____

_____

_____

_____

_____

_____

Skill 14: Apply Prior Knowledge

Apply prior knowledge means that you must use what you already know to help answer a question. The passage will contain information that will be helpful to you. However, you must use this information together with knowledge you already have.

Directions: Read the passage below. The passage is followed by questions that can be answered by applying prior knowledge. Use this passage to answer all the questions on pages 59–61.

THE TOUR DE FRANCE

Do you enjoy riding your bike and are you in good physical condition? Do you like to be physically and mentally challenged? If you answered "yes" to these questions, maybe a grueling bicycle race is in your future. Hope you don't object to overseas travel, because a journey to France is necessary. Begin training immediately and get your travel documents ready.

The Tour de France is regarded as one of the most popular sporting events in the world and is followed intently on television and the Internet by millions of people. The only events followed more closely may be the World Cup in soccer and the Olympics. Initially held in 1903, this 2,400-mile bicycle race is staged annually during July. Portions of the route stay the same from year to year, but other sections are altered. The majority of the course is in France, but racers may also travel through neighboring countries. Lasting about three weeks, it attracts elite bicyclists who cycle through the countryside as well as through towns and villages. Even in the most remote locations, spectators line the road to cheer their favorite riders. For some of the small villages, this is the most exciting event of the year.

The riders compete as teams, and the members of a team develop a cooperative spirit. Sometimes the entire team will assist one of their riders who has the greatest chance of winning the race, since they want one of their team members to succeed. Since this level of racing is so expensive, most of the teams are sponsored by companies. The bikes themselves cost thousands of dollars. Moreover, many of the riders cannot work because they need to train almost full time to prepare for the race.

Only those in excellent physical condition can compete. Some days riders cover relatively flat terrain, but other days they are riding through the Pyrenees and the Alps on mountain roads that are steep enough to give even cars trouble! And there are other challenges. Since the race is conducted in the summer, the temperature can be intense, so an adequate water supply is crucial. And it is probable that the riders will encounter torrential rain at some point during the race.

Since the bicyclists are traveling at extremely high speeds, crashes with other racers can often be disastrous. Disabling injuries are not unusual occurrences. In one race, a bicyclist fell and broke his collarbone on the first day, but he continued and eventually completed the entire distance.

The race is divided into 20 separate sections, known as stages. The five longest stages range from about 130 to 140 miles. Among the stages, there are three medium mountain stages and four high mountain stages. A winner is declared for each stage. Winning a stage is considered a major accomplishment.

After each stage, the rider with the lowest combined time to that point wears a yellow jersey that identifies him as the leader. The winner of the entire tour is the rider with the lowest combined time when the tour finishes in Paris. Thousands of wildly cheering spectators enjoy the spectacular sight of these superb athletes crossing the finish line.

Because of the importance of this race, there are many rules. Failure to strictly follow these can quickly result in disqualification, and ignorance of the rules is no excuse. Here is a small sampling of the rules that are enforced.

- Each team will have nine riders.
- Riders must affix number plates to the front of their bicycles.
- Only official medical personnel can provide medical care.
- Riders may exchange food and drinks with each other.
- Riders from the same team may exchange tires and wheels.
- Riders must follow the official course.
- Riders may not cross railroad crossings when the barrier is down.

If you've decided to wait few years before entering the Tour de France, the next best thing might be traveling to France to watch the race. There are several companies offering such trips. Some offer you an opportunity to ride the identical route as the racers, but at a slower pace. If you want to do this, make your reservations early since these trips are extremely popular. It will be an experience you're sure to remember!

Modeled Instruction

Directions: Below is an example of a question that can be answered by applying prior knowledge. Follow the strategy that is explained to help choose the correct answer.

---

1 What problem is caused by high summer temperatures?

(A) blindness

(B) dehydration

(C) accidents

(D) anxiety

Strategy: First look for information in the passage that can be used to help answer the question. Then, think about what you already know. What you already know should help you to better understand the information in the passage. Choose the answer that makes the most sense to you.

Use this strategy to decide which answer is correct.

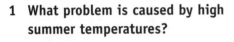 (A) **blindness**

The passage mentions some of the injuries that may occur during the race, but there is no mention of blindness. You already know that hot weather does not cause blindness. Therefore, *choice "A" cannot be the correct answer.*

 (B) **dehydration**

In the paragraph that mentions the high summer temperatures, it states that an adequate water supply is important. Drinking water prevents dehydration. You should know that dehydration is a potential problem during hot weather. Therefore, *choice "B" is the best possible answer.*

(C) **accidents**

The passage notes that there are accidents during the race because of the fast speed. It does not say that the hot weather causes accidents. You know that accidents are not caused by high temperatures. Therefore, *choice "C" cannot be the answer.*

(D) **anxiety**

The passage describes the challenging conditions of the race. The hot weather is a challenge, but no mention is made of it causing anxiety for the highly trained riders. You already know that a professional athlete who is prepared to cycle over mountains will not be anxious about hot weather. Therefore, *choice "D" cannot be the correct answer.*

Guided Instruction

Directions: Use the hints provided to answer the questions below. For question 2, you must choose the correct answer. For question 3, you will need to write out your answer.

2 Tour de France competitors from the United States must have—

Ⓐ a new bike

Ⓑ a valid passport

Ⓒ a map of France

Ⓓ a cheering section

Hint: Consider what may be nice to have, but not necessary. Read the passage for a clue and also use what you know about traveling to a foreign country.

3 If you wanted to ride in the Tour de France, what would your training plan be?

_____
_____
_____
_____
_____
_____
_____
_____
_____
_____
_____
_____
_____
_____
_____
_____

Hint: The passage provides details about the conditions faced by Tour de France riders. It gives information about the distances and the landscape. You know that when training for something you have to be prepared for what lies ahead.

Independent Study

Directions: Answer the following questions on your own. For questions 4, 5, and 6, choose the correct answer. For question 7, you must write out your answer.

4   It is likely that the main challenge for the rider who broke his collarbone was dealing with—

Ⓐ   pain

Ⓑ   cramps

Ⓒ   blisters

Ⓓ   breathlessness

5   What is a Tour de France rider who is not doing well in the race likely to do?

Ⓐ   drop out of the race

Ⓑ   take a different route

Ⓒ   do what he can to help a teammate

Ⓓ   become a member of another team

6   Why is the race called the Tour de France?

Ⓐ   All the riders are French.

Ⓑ   Most of the race route is in France.

Ⓒ   The riders go sightseeing in France.

Ⓓ   The French government pays all expenses.

7   What is the reason for the rule about railroad crossings?

_____

_____

_____

_____

_____

_____

_____

_____

_____

_____

_____

_____

_____

PART B

The 14 Essential Skills for Reading Success

All Together

Section 1:
Modeled Instruction
and Guided Instruction

Each of the fourteen reading comprehension skills are taught all together in this part. Part B is divided into two sections.

Section 1: Modeled Instruction and Guided Instruction

In this section, you will read a passage and answer fourteen questions. The questions will be both multiple-choice and open-ended. Each question covers one of the fourteen essential skills. There will be a *Reminder* to help you remember the strategy needed to answer each question.

Section 2: Independent Study

This section is made up of two themes. Each theme has four passages with fourteen essential skill questions. You are on your own to answer them. There will be different types of passages: stories, biographies, poems, fact-filled material, notes, timelines, letters, and other types of writings. At the end of each theme, there will be three questions about how the passages are connected to their theme. The two themes are:

Theme A: *The Evolution of Communication*

Theme B: *Remarkable American Achievements*

B Section 1: Modeled Instruction and Guided Instruction

The passage in this section is followed by fourteen questions. Each question has a reminder to help you recall which skill you must rely on to answer the question correctly.

Directions: Read the passage below and answer the questions that follow. Use the reminders provided to help you recall the correct strategy for answering each type of question.

DR. MAE JEMISON

Many of us have gazed up at the evening sky and wondered what it would be like to be among the stars and planets. Some of us dream of becoming an astronaut. Others of us say, "When I grow up I want to be a doctor." It's great to have these dreams, but it takes an exceptional individual to make even one of those dreams become a reality, let alone both! Dr. Mae Jemison is just such a person.

Mae Jemison was born in Decatur, Alabama on October 17, 1956, the youngest of three children. Her parents moved the family to Chicago where there were better educational opportunities for their children. At the time, there were not many women studying science. There were also few African-Americans in this field. Mae did not let this lack of role models stop her. She was a strong student who pursued her interests in science and a wide range of other subjects. She showed drive and determination at an early age.

Mae graduated from Morgan Park High School near the top of her class. She entered Stanford University at the age of 16 and graduated with a degree in Chemical Engineering. Because of her *divergent* interests, Mae could not confine herself to one area of study. She also earned a degree in Afro-American Studies.

Mae had become interested in medicine. She attended Cornell University Medical College and graduated as a medical doctor in 1981. Always interested in the world around her, she traveled widely. Mae decided to work in the Peace Corps in Africa from 1983 through 1985. She supervised many members of the medical staff. Mae also worked on developing new vaccines for diseases that affected many people in that part of the world.

After returning from the Peace Corps, Mae began working as a doctor in California. At the same time, she started taking classes in engineering. Then she decided to apply to become an astronaut. In 1985 Dr. Jemison and 14 other applicants were chosen. The qualifications for acceptance are among the most rigorous for any program. These select few were chosen from among 2,000 people!

The training to become an astronaut is very demanding. You must be in top physical condition. You must learn to perform well under great stress. Some people are unable to complete the training. Mae persevered and in August of 1988 she became the first black female astronaut. On September 12, 1992, she traveled on the space shuttle *Endeavor*. This was a joint mission with Japanese astronauts. As a Science Mission Specialist, Dr. Jemison conducted and supervised many experiments. Important discoveries resulted from the work of Mae and the other astronauts.

In the years that followed the flight, Dr. Jemison pursued her desire to teach. She was a professor at Dartmouth College and also taught courses at Cornell University. In 1994 she founded The Earth We Share, a science camp for students from around the world.

Dr. Jemison also started several businesses. One company develops devices to help people under stress. It is hoped this equipment can also be used to help astronauts avoid motion sickness. Many people are interested in the possible uses for her products.

Mae Jemison working on a microgravity experiment onboard the STS-47 Spacelab J, September 12, 1992. Photo courtesy of NASA.

Along with her teaching and business interests, Mae found the time to write a book. In 2001 her autobiography, *Find Where the Wind Goes: Moments from My Life* was published. Undoubtedly, many people were inspired by her story.

Dr. Jemison has received many honors. In 2001 she was elected into the National Academy of Sciences' Institute of Medicine. She was also inducted into the National Women's Hall of Fame and received honorary degrees from several universities. She is truly a remarkable person!

From an early age, Dr. Mae Jemison always believed in following her dreams. She would let no obstacles stand in her way. She is committed to passing that belief to the next generation. She wants to encourage women and minorities to become involved with science. Mae travels around the country speaking to many groups. The audience enjoys hearing her words of encouragement and inspiration.

"Don't let anyone rob you of your imagination, your creativity,
or your curiosity. It's your place in the world; it's your life. Go on and do all you can
with it, and make it the life you want to live." –Mae Jemison

Directions: Answer the following questions using the reminders provided to help you recall the correct strategy for answering each type of question.

Recall Facts and Details

1 **How long was Dr. Jemison in the Peace Corps?**

Ⓐ 6 years

Ⓑ 4 years

Ⓒ 2 years

Ⓓ 5 years

Reminder: The answer to this question can be found right in the passage. Look for key words. Read the sentences with these key words very carefully to find the detail or fact needed to answer the question correctly.

Identify Main Idea

2 **What would be a good title for this passage? Explain your answer.**

_____

_____

_____

_____

_____

_____

_____

_____

_____

Reminder: The main idea is what the whole story is about. To answer this question correctly you need to think about the entire passage, not just one part.

Identify Sequence

3 **According to the passage, when did Mae study chemical engineering?**

Ⓐ after she became a doctor

Ⓑ before she went to Cornell

Ⓒ before she moved to Chicago

Ⓓ after she received an honorary degree

Reminder: Find each of the answer choices within the passage. You can make a timeline to help you choose the correct answer.

Analyze Language and Vocabulary

4 **In the third paragraph, the author of the passage uses the word *divergent* to mean—**

Ⓐ early

Ⓑ similar

Ⓒ difficult

Ⓓ different

Reminder: This type of question asks you to identify the meaning of a word. To find the meaning of a word you must think about how the word is used in the passage.

Analyze Character, Plot, and Setting

5 **From what you learn of her in the passage, how would you describe Dr. Jemison?**

_____

_____

_____

_____

_____

_____

_____

_____

_____

_____

_____

Reminder: To answer this type of question you must think about a character in the passage. Consider the actions of the character and the events that take place.

Recognize Cause and Effect

> **6 Why did the Jemison family move to Chicago?**
>
> Ⓐ The housing was more affordable in Chicago.
>
> Ⓑ Mae was having trouble with some classmates.
>
> Ⓒ There were better job opportunities for Mae's father.
>
> Ⓓ Her parents wanted Mae to receive a better education.

Reminder: Cause and effect go together. To answer this type of question you must find the event or action in the answer choice that goes with the event or action in the question.

Compare and Contrast

> **7 Mae and the other astronauts were similar because they all—**
>
> Ⓐ were able to lift heavy objects
>
> Ⓑ were doctors and engineers
>
> Ⓒ had excellent qualifications
>
> Ⓓ had many honorary degrees

Reminder: Compare questions ask you to tell how things are alike. Contrast questions ask you to tell how things are different. Use details from the passage to help you choose the correct answer.

Distinguish Fact from Opinion

> **8 Which of the following is an opinion NOT a fact?**
>
> Ⓐ Dr. Jemison was born in Alabama.
>
> Ⓑ The audience enjoys hearing her words.
>
> Ⓒ Mae found time to write her autobiography.
>
> Ⓓ She enrolled at Cornell University Medical College.

Reminder To answer this question you must be able to identify which answer choices are facts and which one is an opinion. Facts can be proven true, opinions cannot.

Predict Outcomes

> **9 What will Dr. Jemison will probably do in the future?**
>
> Ⓐ continue giving lectures
>
> Ⓑ retire from all her activities
>
> Ⓒ write another autobiography
>
> Ⓓ teach elementary school in Alabama

Reminder To predict an outcome you must use information in the story to decide what you think will happen next. More than one answer may seem possible. You must choose the best answer.

Draw Conclusions

10 **Which of the following is a valid statement based on the information in this passage?**

(A) Many people apply to medical school.

(B) Mae has varied supervisory experience.

(C) All Japanese astronauts enjoy working with Mae.

(D) Mae was unhappy about the family leaving Alabama.

Reminder: To draw conclusions you must think about many different facts and details found in the passage. The passage does not tell you the answer, but it does give you the information you need to draw a conclusion.

Make Inferences

11 **The fact that Mae started her camp shows that—**

(A) she didn't have enough things to do

(B) she cares a great deal about young people

(C) she is always anxious to try something new

(D) she thinks young people are not motivated

Reminder: Facts and details in a passage can suggest an answer without actually stating the answer. These questions are asking you to infer the meaning of events or details.

Analyze Point of View and Purpose

12 **In the first paragraph, the author sets the tone for the rest of the passage by—**

(A) discussing nighttime activities

(B) asking if you want to become a doctor

(C) contrasting Dr. Jemison to most people

(D) stating how difficult it is to be a success

Reminder: How the author feels about a topic is a point of view. Why the author wrote a passage is the purpose. Details in a passage often suggest a point of view or purpose.

Identify Literary Forms and Sources of Information

13 **You might expect to find this passage in a book titled—**

(A) *Famous Doctors*

(B) *Getting an Education*

(C) *Women of Distinction*

(D) *Becoming an Astronaut*

Reminder: To answer this question you must think about what type of information you would expect to find in different types of writing. Each literary form has certain features that help identify it.

Analyze Point of View and Purpose

14 Why is Dr. Jemison probably an outstanding teacher?

_____

_____

_____

_____

Reminder: The answer to this question cannot be found in the passage alone. In addition to details from the passage, you must use your own knowledge to help answer the question.

_____

_____

_____

_____

_____

_____

_____

_____

_____

_____

_____

_____

_____

_____

_____

_____

_____

_____

PART B

The 14 Essential Skills for Reading Success

All Together

Part B | Section 2: Independent Study

This section is made up of two themes. Each theme has four passages with fourteen essential skill questions. You are on your own to answer them. There are different types of passages: stories, biographies, poems, fact-filled material, notes, timelines, letters, and other types of writings. At the end of each theme, there will be three questions about how the passages are connected to their theme. The two themes are:

Theme A: *The Evolution of Communication*
    Selection 1: *Communication through the Ages*
    Selection 2: *A Treasured Antique*
    Selection 3: *Who Invented the Radio?*
    Selection 4: *A Blackout Has Benefits*

Theme B: *Remarkable American Achievements*
    Selection 1: *A Desert Landmark*
    Selection 2: *Mount Rushmore National Memorial*
    Selection 3: *Portland Head Light*
    Selection 4: *A Stop on the Freedom Trail*

Section 2: Independent Study

There are two groups of passages in this Section. Each group is made up of four passages. The four passages are thematically linked. They are written about a single theme. This is the first theme.

Theme A: The Evolution of Communication

Selection 1 | **Directions:** Read the passage below and answer the questions that follow.

Communication through the Ages

The word "communicate" means to pass along information. Human beings have always wanted to communicate with each other. The earliest people probably used simple gestures and sounds. Over time, sounds were used to form languages. This made it possible for people to share more complex ideas.

Tens of thousands of years ago, people painted pictures on rocks and in caves to tell stories about their lives. The Egyptians used symbols and pictures to record information on the walls of the pyramids. Symbols and pictures were eventually replaced by alphabets.

Once paper was invented, it was much easier to write messages and record important information. Paper was also easy to carry and could be sent great distances. The invention of the printing press was another significant improvement. People could record large amounts of information on paper. Many copies could be made. It was much more practical than writing it all by hand!

Now that people were writing letters and printing materials, they had to find ways to move them from one place to another. In the United States during the Colonial times, people asked friends and traveling merchants to deliver their letters, books, and documents. Later the Pony Express served this purpose. In 1861 the Pony Express carried President Abraham Lincoln's speech across the country. It took seven days and seventeen hours.

During the 1800s the telegraph machine was invented. Now it was possible to communicate across great distances by sending electrical signals over wires. For the first time in history, messages were *transmitted* instead of transported. Samuel Morse developed a code to represent different letters of the alphabet. This improved communication using the telegraph. By the end of the century, the invention of the telephone made long-distance communication even easier. Alexander Graham Bell's name is usually connected with the telephone, but Antonio Meucci invented it.

— **3500s B.C.E.** People used pictures and symbols

— **1500s B.C.E.** First alphabet developed

— **105 B.C.E.** Paper invented in China

— **1454** Guttenberg built a printing press

— **1831** Electric telegraph invented

— **1876** Bell introduced telephone in the United States

— **1901** Marconi sent first radio waves across the Atlantic Ocean

— **1925** First television signals transmitted

— **1969** Computers linked to form Internet

— **1994** World Wide Web became available

Changes continued during the 1900s. First came the radio. Later the invention of television made it possible to transmit images. People could now see, as well as hear, what was happening around the world. Telephones were improved. The touch-tone phone was developed in 1963. Next came the cordless phone that allowed people to talk to each other while walking around their homes. And then the cellular phone that let them have conversations from almost any location. The invention of computers was followed by development of the Internet and then the World Wide Web.

Less than a hundred years ago, it took a letter three weeks to get from Maine to Georgia. Now it takes seconds to send an e-mail across a continent. This is an amazing achievement.

Communication has always been important to people. New inventions have improved the way we communicate and these advances will continue. People living one hundred years ago could not have imagined that there would be a thing called e-mail. How do you think people will be able to communicate one hundred years from now?

Directions: Answer the following questions on your own.

1   When did people first begin to communicate with each other?

Ⓐ   when paper was invented

Ⓑ   when this happened is not known

Ⓒ   when the electric phone was invented

Ⓓ   when the first alphabet was developed

2   Which of the following sentences fits best in the third paragraph of this passage?

Ⓐ   Ink was made from paint and dye.

Ⓑ   Books could be printed more quickly.

Ⓒ   Johannes Guttenberg was a German craftsman.

Ⓓ   Chester Carlson created a photocopier for office use.

3   Which of the following events happened before the first radio waves were sent across the Atlantic Ocean?

Ⓐ   Television was invented.

Ⓑ   The touch-tone telephone was invented.

Ⓒ   Morse code was developed.

Ⓓ   The Internet improved communication.

4   Read the sentence below from the passage.

"For the first time in history, messages were transmitted instead of transported."

What does the word *transmitted* mean as it is used in this sentence?

Ⓐ   shown to everyone in the world

Ⓑ   made into pictures

Ⓒ   sent across the ocean

Ⓓ   sent out as electric signals

5   Who invented the telephone?

Ⓐ   Bell

Ⓑ   Meucci

Ⓒ   Lincoln

Ⓓ   Guttenberg

6 Which of the following events led to Morse code being developed?

   Ⓐ The telephone was introduced.

   Ⓑ The electric telegraph was invented.

   Ⓒ Computers were connected to create the Internet.

   Ⓓ Radio waves were sent across the Atlantic Ocean.

7 Compare the telegraph and the telephone. Explain one way they are alike and one way they are different.

_____

_____

_____

_____

_____

_____

_____

_____

_____

_____

_____

_____

_____

_____

8 Which of the following statements from the passage is an example of an opinion?

   Ⓐ Paper was easy to transport.

   Ⓑ These advances will continue.

   Ⓒ Samuel Morse developed a code.

   Ⓓ Bell introduced the telephone in the United States.

9 Which of the following would most likely be true if the Internet did not exist?

   Ⓐ There would be no computers.

   Ⓑ People would not communicate.

   Ⓒ People would not use telephones.

   Ⓓ There would be no World Wide Web.

10 Why was the invention of television important?

   Ⓐ For the first time, information was transmitted instead of transported.

   Ⓑ It proved that electricity could be used to send signals across the Atlantic Ocean.

   Ⓒ It allowed people to hear what was happening all around the world for the very first time.

   Ⓓ It allowed people to see what was happening all around the world for the very first time.

11 Explain two ways that paper improved the way people could communicate. Base your answer on details from the passage.

_____

_____

_____

_____

_____

_____

_____

_____

_____

_____

_____

_____

_____

_____

_____

_____

_____

_____

_____

_____

12 The main purpose of this passage is to—

Ⓐ state an opinion

Ⓑ inform the reader

Ⓒ entertain the reader

Ⓓ compare and contrast

13 This passage can best be described as—

Ⓐ a biography

Ⓑ a work of fiction

Ⓒ historical facts

Ⓓ scientific research

14 Which of the following would you use to communicate with someone living far away if there were no electricity?

Ⓐ a letter

Ⓑ an e-mail

Ⓒ Morse code

Ⓓ a phone call

Selection 2 | Directions: Read the passage below and answer the questions that follow.

A Treasured Antique

Calvin's mother called up the stairs urging him to hurry up, so he hastened to conclude the e-mail. At least once a month he corresponded with his cousin, Debra. Calvin knew she was probably wondering why his e-mail was so long overdue, so he had explained that his newspaper delivery job was keeping him busy.

Debra lived in California and Calvin lived in Maine, so they communicated by e-mail. Whenever something exciting occurred, Calvin would sit at the computer and start typing. Calvin enjoyed telling Debra about what was happening on the east coast and, in return, Debra would update Calvin about west coast events.

Calvin finished typing the last sentence and sent the e-mail. In a few seconds, it would be in Debra's inbox. Turning off his computer, he raced down the stairs, out the door, and into the car where his mother was waiting with the engine running.

Fortunately, there was very little traffic, so they were not delayed. Just a few minutes later, Calvin and his mother arrived at their *destination,* and walked up the cobblestone path. Before Calvin could knock, the front door swung open.

"What took so long?" Grandpa inquired, as he gave them each a hug. "I was about to start cleaning out the attic by myself. But I was under strict orders from the two of you not to do any heavy lifting."

Calvin explained to his grandfather about the e-mail he sent to Debra. He was still feeling guilty about not having written in such a long time. He admitted that to his grandfather and explained about his new job.

His grandfather reassured him that his cousin would understand and then observed, "If they had e-mail when I was your age, I would have saved a lot of money on stamps. And I wouldn't have taken all those walks to the post office."

Then the three of them made their way up the steep, creaking steps to the attic. Grandpa, the first to reach the top step, jerked on a string and the lights came on. Peering around the attic, they saw piles of boxes covered with dust and fluttering cobwebs dangling from the wooden beams overhead.

"Let's get started," Grandpa suggested. "The truck will be here in less than an hour to pick up all this junk."

Calvin knew that Grandpa loved to save things. Grandpa would always tell Calvin, "There are memories attached to everything." But even Grandpa realized that his attic was becoming too cluttered. He had already sorted through all of the boxes to find the items that he treasured most, and placed these special items in an old trunk in his bedroom, a much better place for them. What remained was going to be carted away.

Calvin and his mother worked together lifting the heavy boxes, while Grandpa carried the lighter boxes to the front curb. Finally, there was only one box left but, as Calvin bent to lift it, he noticed an object on a small table near the attic window. Straightening up, Calvin walked toward the window. A few seconds later, hearing his exclamation of surprise, his grandfather joined him.

"Now, how did I forget about that?" Grandpa said, shaking his head in disbelief.

Calvin had never seen a typewriter like this one before. He remembered seeing his mother use an electric typewriter. When she pressed on the keys of the typewriter a wheel with different letters would strike an ink ribbon and ink would be transferred from the ribbon onto a piece of paper. Grandpa's typewriter looked similar, but not the same and it appeared to be very old. Instead of a wheel with letters, it had several long bars with letters. Also, it did not have a switch to turn it on and off. However, it did have an ink ribbon similar to the one on his mother's old typewriter.

For many years Grandpa had been a newspaper journalist who reported on events around the world. Grandpa told Calvin that he remembered writing the very first story of his career on this very typewriter, and that this ancient machine was one of his most prized possessions. Observing Calvin's excitement, Grandpa scratched his head and thought for a moment as he gazed at his grandson. Grandpa knew how much Calvin loved to write. *I wonder if my old typewriter is ready to record some new ideas,* he chuckled to himself.

"I'm not sure where I'm going to find room for that typewriter around here," Grandpa stated. "Do you happen to know a place where we can put it?" he inquired with a big smile. "Any suggestions?"

Smiling back, Calvin gave his grandfather a big hug.

Directions: Answer the following questions on your own.

1 Why did Calvin go to his grandfather's house?

Ⓐ to pack some boxes

Ⓑ to have lunch with him

Ⓒ to help him clean the attic

Ⓓ to help him find his typewriter

2 What would be another good title for this story?

Ⓐ "Lost Memories"

Ⓑ "A Box of Treasures"

Ⓒ "Calvin Sends an E-mail"

Ⓓ "A Day at Grandpa's House"

3 What does Calvin do before he goes to Grandpa's house?

Ⓐ He finds a typewriter.

Ⓑ He drops a letter in the mailbox.

Ⓒ He sends an e-mail to his cousin.

Ⓓ He carries a box down the stairs.

4 Read the sentence below from the passage.

"A few minutes later, Calvin and his mother arrived at their destination."

What does the word *destination* mean as it is used in this sentence?

Ⓐ a place that is very pleasant

Ⓑ a place that no one wants to visit

Ⓒ a place that someone has just been

Ⓓ a place to which someone is going

5 How would you describe Grandpa's attic? Base your answer on details from the passage.

_____

_____

_____

_____

6 How does Grandpa react when Calvin finds the typewriter in the attic?

Ⓐ He is sad.

Ⓑ He is angry.

Ⓒ He is happy.

Ⓓ He is surprised.

_____

_____

_____

_____

_____

_____

_____

_____

7 How is the typewriter that Calvin finds in Grandpa's attic different from the one his mother used to have?

Ⓐ It is an electric typewriter.

Ⓑ It does not have an ink ribbon.

Ⓒ It uses a wheel with letters to print on paper.

Ⓓ It does not have a switch to turn it on and off.

8 Which of the following statements from the passage is NOT considered a fact?

Ⓐ "Calvin knew that Grandpa loved to save things."

Ⓑ "Grandpa used to be a newspaper journalist."

Ⓒ "The truck will be here in less than an hour."

Ⓓ "The bedroom was a much better place for them."

9 What will most likely happen with the typewriter Calvin found in the attic?

Ⓐ Grandpa will leave it in the attic.

Ⓑ Grandpa will give it to Calvin to take home.

Ⓒ Grandpa will take it to a shop to be fixed.

Ⓓ Grandpa will ask Calvin to take it to the curb.

10 Why was the e-mail Calvin sent to Debra so long overdue?

Ⓐ Calvin was too tired to write.

Ⓑ Calvin was away on vacation.

Ⓒ Calvin had been busy with his job.

Ⓓ Calvin had been studying for a test.

11 You can tell that Grandpa has not cleaned the attic in a long time by the fact that—

Ⓐ there are a lot of boxes

Ⓑ he left the typewriter there

Ⓒ he had to turn on the light

Ⓓ the boxes are covered with dust

12 With which of the following statements would Grandpa mostly likely agree?

Ⓐ Things were made much better years ago.

Ⓑ All personal belongings can be easily replaced.

Ⓒ Things do not have to be expensive to be valuable.

Ⓓ You should not bother to save things when they get old.

13 This passage is an example of—

Ⓐ a novel

Ⓑ a myth

Ⓒ a short story

Ⓓ a folk tale

14 Read the sentence below from the passage.

"Grandpa would always tell Calvin, 'There are memories attached to everything.'"

Explain what Grandpa means by this statement. Base your answer on details from the passage and your own experiences.

_____

_____

_____

_____

_____

_____

_____

_____

_____

_____

_____

_____

Who Invented the Radio?

Little girl listening to the radio, circa 1920s. Photo courtesy of the National Archives.

Radio is a very important means of communication. It has become a part of our daily life. The radio has made it possible for people to communicate with each other over great distances. From the 1920s to the 1950s, people used radios in much the same way as televisions are used today. Millions of families would gather around a radio to listen to entertaining programs and music. They would also listen to the radio for the news. They could learn what was happening around the world much more quickly than they could before radio was invented. Radio is still popular today. Now there are car radios, portable radios, and headsets. People can listen to the radio almost anywhere.

Radios have many important uses. There are radios that allow airplane pilots, police officers, sailors, and others to communicate over long distances. Scientists use radio waves to learn about the weather.

HENRY
1797–1878

FARADAY
1791–1821

MAXWELL
1831–1879

A radio works by changing sounds or other signals into radio waves. These radio waves can travel at the speed of light. This means they can travel 186,282 miles in one second!

Many people contributed to the development of the radio. In the early 1830s, Joseph Henry, a college professor in the United States, and Michael Faraday, a scientist in England were conducting research and *formulating* theories. Working independently, each developed the same theory: electricity in one wire can produce electricity in another wire, even though the two wires are not connected. About 30 years later, another scientist named James Maxwell used their theory to come to the conclusion that electromagnetic waves did exist. Heinrich Hertz, a German scientist, later performed experiments to prove that this was true.

At about the same time, Nikola Tesla began experimenting with electrical motors, coils, and other devices. Many of the things he used were similar to those that are used in today's radios and televisions. Tesla, an inventor, developed the concepts and built a model radio. But it was Guglielmo Marconi who developed the first working radio.

Marconi, an Italian scientist, had studied the experiments that were performed with electromagnetic waves. He began his own laboratory experiments and succeeded in sending a wireless signal over a distance of one and a half miles. It became known as wireless telegraphy. Today, it is called a radio.

Marconi continued his experiments. In 1899 he transmitted a signal more than 60 miles to a boat at sea. This was an important step. It proved that electromagnetic waves were able to follow the curve of Earth's surface. This meant that wireless telegraphy could be used over even greater distances. In 1901 Marconi sent a wireless signal from England to Canada. This was the first wireless communication across the Atlantic Ocean.

Marconi was awarded the Nobel Prize in physics in 1901. He certainly deserves credit for being the first person to succeed at using wireless communication. But Tesla had demonstrated the basic principles and built the first model radio. He did that years before Marconi began his experiments. In 1943 the United States Supreme Court recognized Nikola Tesla as the inventor of the radio.

The debate over who invented the radio still continues. Perhaps the radio, like so many other inventions, should be viewed as a group effort. Many people have built upon each other's work. Many have added their own contributions. Today's cell phones are just one example of how wireless communication continues to change. Undoubtedly more improvements lie ahead, but only time will tell.

HERTZ
1857–1894

TESLA
1856–1943

MARCONI
1874–1937

Directions: Answer the following questions on your own.

1   Who was successful at sending the first wireless signal?

   Ⓐ Nikola Tesla

   Ⓑ Joseph Henry

   Ⓒ Heinrich Hertz

   Ⓓ Guglielmo Marconi

2   What is this passage mostly about?

   Ⓐ how the radio became popular

   Ⓑ the world's greatest scientists

   Ⓒ the history of communication

   Ⓓ people who helped to invent the radio

3   Which of the following happened after Marconi won the Nobel Prize?

   Ⓐ Marconi built the first working radio.

   Ⓑ Tesla was given credit for inventing the radio.

   Ⓒ Hertz proved the existence of electromagnetic waves.

   Ⓓ Henry developed the same theory as Faraday.

4   Read the statement below from the passage.

   Joseph Henry and Michael Faraday were conducting research and formulating theories.

   What does the word *formulating* **mean as it is used in this sentence?**

   Ⓐ arguing

   Ⓑ printing

   Ⓒ drawing

   Ⓓ developing

5   The first wireless communication across the Atlantic Ocean was sent from—

   Ⓐ Canada to Italy

   Ⓑ England to Italy

   Ⓒ England to Canada

   Ⓓ France to Canada

6   Which of the following events caused James Maxwell to conclude that electromagnetic waves existed?

   Ⓐ Tesla built electrical motors.

   Ⓑ Hertz proved electromagnetic waves existed.

   Ⓒ Marconi used wireless telegraphy to communicate.

   Ⓓ Faraday and Henry developed a theory about electrical currents.

7 Explain how the radio was at one time similar to television. Use details from the passage to support your answer.

_____

_____

_____

_____

_____

_____

_____

_____

_____

_____

_____

_____

_____

_____

_____

_____

_____

_____

_____

_____

_____

_____

_____

_____

8 **Which of the following statements from the passage is an example of an opinion?**

   Ⓐ Scientists use radio waves to learn about the weather.

   Ⓑ Perhaps the radio, like so many other inventions, should be viewed as a group effort.

   Ⓒ There are radios that allow airplane pilots, police officers, sailors, and others to communicate over long distances.

   Ⓓ Today's cell phones are just one example of how wireless communication continues to change.

---

9 **Which of the following will most likely happen in the future?**

   Ⓐ Radios will replace televisions in most homes.

   Ⓑ Tesla will be awarded the Nobel Prize in physics.

   Ⓒ Marconi will be given credit for inventing the radio.

   Ⓓ People will continue to invent new ways to communicate.

---

10 **Why is the invention of wireless communication important?**

   Ⓐ People could listen to music.

   Ⓑ It eliminated the need for telegraphy.

   Ⓒ It made it possible to communicate using sound.

   Ⓓ It made communication over great distances possible.

---

11 **Why did the Supreme Court state that Tesla was the inventor of the radio?**

   Ⓐ He did most of the work.

   Ⓑ He was smarter than Marconi.

   Ⓒ He experimented with coils used to make radios.

   Ⓓ He created the first model based on concepts he developed.

12 Why does the author of this passage believe that inventing the radio was a group effort? Base your answer on details from the passage.

_____

_____

_____

_____

_____

_____

_____

_____

_____

_____

_____

_____

_____

_____

_____

_____

_____

_____

13 What type of book should you read to learn more about Nikola Tesla?

Ⓐ a novel

Ⓑ an atlas

Ⓒ a dictionary

Ⓓ a biography

14 Which of the following is an example of wireless telegraphy?

Ⓐ A person listens to the radio in a car.

Ⓑ A person sends an e-mail using a computer.

Ⓒ A person plays a video game using a television.

Ⓓ A person mails a letter to someone who lives far away.

Theme A: The Evolution of Communication

Selection 4 | **Directions:** Read the passage below and answer the questions that follow.

A Blackout Has Benefits

Dear Tanya,

I hope you enjoyed your first day of school. Things are not the same around here since you moved. It would not be so bad if you only moved a few blocks away, but Florida is so far from North Dakota. At least you have a warmer climate. It is already starting to get cold back here.

If you are wondering why I am writing instead of sending an e-mail, the answer is that there's no electricity in our neighborhood. Lightning struck a power generator and caused a blackout. Right now it is already dark outside, so I'm "penning my missive" by the light of a candle on the desk in my bedroom. I thought I'd use some old-fashioned language to match the mood. The illumination the candle provides isn't very satisfactory, but the flickering shadows it casts are fascinating.

So many things are different without electricity. Instead of watching television, most of the neighbors are out in front of their houses having conversations and socializing. Some people are listening to the news about the power outage on their battery-operated radios. It is very serene and quiet tonight.

Sitting here writing this letter makes me realize how much we take for granted. Think about how lucky we are that we can communicate with each other using e-mail. Imagine if we lived in a time before there was electricity.

Remember when we read the book about the Pony Express in our social studies class? It said that it took riders about ten days to deliver mail from California to Missouri. That seems like a long time to wait for an important message. And in those days if someone wanted to send a letter to a friend in Europe, it would go by boat! Can you imagine how long that would take? When I mail this letter, you'll receive it in a couple of days and if you lived in Europe it would go by plane and arrive almost as quickly. And, of course, with e-mail you receive my message a few seconds after I send it.

In addition to e-mail being faster than the Pony Express, it's a whole lot easier for everyone involved. You and I click a couple of keys and that's it. But the Pony Express utilized about 400 horses and required almost 200 mail stations. To make the horses' burden as light as possible, the riders had to weigh less than 125 pounds, so doesn't it seem possible that many were teenagers? In fact, I seem to recall that the youngest rider was only 11 years old! I'm sure riding a pony across the country through all kinds of weather was fatiguing work, but it must have been a thrilling adventure, too. The Pony Express only lasted about two years, but in that time only one sack of mail was lost, so those riders did an admirable job.

I've become so accustomed to the speed and convenience of e-mail. But I realize as I sit here using a pen to write this letter to you that this whole experience is rather gratifying. It seems more personal and friendly. I enjoyed selecting the writing paper, and did you notice that I used a pen with colored ink that matched the design on the stationery? It was an opportunity for a bit of artistic expression. Maybe you should give it a try the next time you want to send me a message.

I guess having this blackout wasn't such a bad thing after all. It really helped to shed some light (sorry, that's a terrible pun!) on a few things. Writing this letter to you has made me realize just how much fun it can be to sit at a desk and pen a letter by candlelight. From now on I think I will try to write a letter at least once a week, so don't forget to check your mailbox every now and then.

I'll end this letter now so I can seal it in an envelope, address the envelope, and put on a stamp. Tomorrow I'll drop it in the mailbox on the corner. Writing all that reminds me just how easy e-mail is!

I hope you enjoy things at your new school. Tell your mom and dad I said hello. I am looking forward to visiting you and your family next summer.

Your friend,
Yasmeen

Directions: Answer the following questions on your own.

1 Where was Yasmeen when she wrote this letter?

Ⓐ in Florida

Ⓑ in her bedroom

Ⓒ in front of her house

Ⓓ in a school classroom

2 The fifth paragraph in this letter is mostly about—

Ⓐ traveling across the country

Ⓑ the first Pony Express journey

Ⓒ using e-mail to send a message

Ⓓ how communication has changed

3 Study the timeline below.

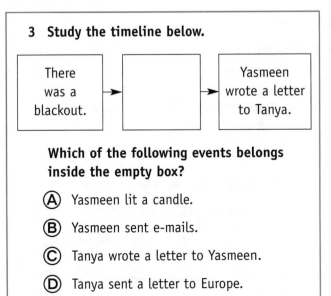

Which of the following events belongs inside the empty box?

Ⓐ Yasmeen lit a candle.

Ⓑ Yasmeen sent e-mails.

Ⓒ Tanya wrote a letter to Yasmeen.

Ⓓ Tanya sent a letter to Europe.

4 Read the sentences below from the passage.

"I guess having this blackout wasn't such a bad thing after all. It really helped to shed some light on a few things."

What do these sentences tell the reader?

Ⓐ Yasmeen enjoys sitting in the dark.

Ⓑ Yasmeen believes having a blackout is a lot of fun.

Ⓒ Yasmeen does not think it is very dark even with the blackout.

Ⓓ Yasmeen believes she has learned something from the experience.

5 Who is Tanya?

Ⓐ Yasmeen's sister

Ⓑ Yasmeen's aunt

Ⓒ Yasmeen's friend

Ⓓ Yasmeen's cousin

6 Why did Yasmeen decide to write a letter to Tanya instead of sending an e-mail?

(A) Tanya's computer was broken.

(B) There was no electricity in her area.

(C) Yasmeen had never written a letter before.

(D) Tanya lived too far away to send an e-mail.

7 How is writing a letter different from sending someone an e-mail? Use details from the letter to support your answer.

_____

_____

_____

_____

_____

_____

_____

_____

_____

_____

_____

_____

_____

_____

_____

_____

8 Which of the following statements from the passage is an example of an opinion?

(A) "The Pony Express only lasted about two years."

(B) "Tomorrow I'll drop it in the mailbox on the corner."

(C) "Most of the neighbors are out in front of their houses."

(D) "I guess having this blackout wasn't such a bad thing after all."

9 In the future, Yasmeen will most likely—

(A) stop corresponding with Tanya

(B) write letters and send e-mail to Tanya

(C) use only e-mail to communicate with Tanya

(D) only write letters to communicate with Tanya

10 From reading this passage you can tell that—

(A) Yasmeen lives in Florida

(B) Tanya just moved to Europe

(C) Yasmeen just moved to Florida

(D) Tanya used to live in North Dakota

11 Why does Yasmeen think that she and Tanya are lucky to be able to send each other e-mail? Base your answer on details in the letter.

_____

_____

_____

_____

_____

_____

_____

_____

_____

_____

_____

_____

_____

_____

_____

_____

12 Which of the following is NOT a reason why Yasmeen wrote this letter?

Ⓐ to tell Tanya about what she just learned at school

Ⓑ to tell Tanya about the blackout that had occurred

Ⓒ to tell Tanya that things are not the same since she moved

Ⓓ to tell Tanya how much she is looking forward to visiting next summer

13 Which of the following would be the best source of information to use if you wanted to learn more about the Pony Express?

Ⓐ a book about the history of America

Ⓑ a book about modern communication

Ⓒ a newspaper article about e-mail

Ⓓ a Web site about horse training

14 Which of the following is most similar to sending a message by Pony Express?

Ⓐ sending an e-mail to someone

Ⓑ sending a telegram to someone

Ⓒ sending a letter through the mail

Ⓓ using a fax machine to send a message

Theme Questions

Directions: The first theme of Section 2 was, "The Evolution of Communication." Answer these questions. They are about the four Theme A selections you just read.

---

1 **Which of the following would be most helpful if you needed to send a message quickly to someone who lives far away?**

Ⓐ a typewriter

Ⓑ a telegraph

Ⓒ a piece of paper

Ⓓ a printing press

---

2 **Choose any invention mentioned in the passages you have read. Explain how this invention helped to improve the way people communicate. Support your answer with details from the passages.**

_____

_____

_____

_____

_____

_____

_____

_____

_____

_____

_____

_____

_____

_____

3 Why is communication important? Base your answer on your own experiences and details from the passages.

_____

_____

_____

_____

_____

_____

_____

_____

_____

_____

_____

_____

_____

_____

_____

_____

_____

_____

_____

_____

_____

_____

_____

_____

_____

_____

_____

_____

Section 2: Independent Study

This is the second theme for Part B. This theme is also made up of four passages.

Theme B: Remarkable American Achievements

Selection 1 | Directions: Read the passage below and answer the questions that follow.

A Desert Landmark

Construction of Hoover Dam, Boulder City, Nevada, 1933; Aerial view of the Hoover Dam, 1972. Photos courtesy of the National Archives.

When most tourists travel to Nevada, they are heading for Las Vegas. The bright lights and excitement are a major draw. Every year, however, millions of visitors from around the world also venture about 30 miles out of this city. They visit an engineering marvel, the Hoover Dam, which is on the Arizona-Nevada state line. It is a trip worth taking.

Arizona, California, Colorado, Nevada, New Mexico, Utah, and Wyoming are arid states. Early in the last century, it became apparent that they needed to find a way to share the waters of the Colorado River system. They also had to agree on a way to produce electricity. The 1928 Boulder Canyon Project Act included the building of the Hoover Dam. The bill approving the project was signed into law just a few weeks before Herbert Hoover became president. His administration had the task of seeing that the work got done. Hoover played a large role in getting the states to come to an agreement about how the water would be shared.

Many experts credit the growth of these states in large measure to the building of the dam. Today there are cities and farming areas that would not exist if the dam hadn't been built. Increasing numbers of Americans migrate to the Southwest to live, work, or retire.

This famous landmark on the Colorado River rises 726.4 feet above the water. The Hoover Dam weighs about 6.6 million tons and is able to hold back the waters of one of the United States' mightiest rivers. Astronauts in space shuttles have reported that they can see this landmark. It's that big!

The structure is made of more than three million cubic yards of concrete, which is obviously a lot of concrete. But how can you get a sense of how big it is? Pretend for a moment that all the concrete in the dam could be used to construct a building. That building would be taller than the Empire State Building in New York City. If you could use the concrete to build a highway sixteen-feet wide, it would stretch from San Francisco to New York.

On average, 3,500 people worked on this project during the five-year construction of Hoover Dam, which began in 1931. It was a great challenge just to supply food and water to this many people. At the height of activity in June 1934, 5,218 people were on the payroll. In fact, a whole new town called Boulder City was built to house the workers and their families. Today, Boulder City is a *thriving* community.

The first residents of Boulder City worked for five years to complete the dam and its power plant. But that was not all they accomplished. A 22.7-mile railroad line and a seven-mile highway were also constructed. And a 222-mile-long power line was built. The last concrete for the dam was poured in May 1935. All the dam's features were completed by March 1, 1936. That was almost two years ahead of schedule! It was an amazing accomplishment.

Although it's known as Hoover Dam today, this was not always the case. For many years the dam was called "Boulder Dam." Politics may have been the reason for this name change. After Hoover left office, Harold Ickes was the Secretary of the Interior in the administration of Franklin Roosevelt. Ickes, who did not like Mr. Hoover, began referring to the dam as "Boulder Dam." The nation followed his example. However, some people disagreed with Ickes. In 1947 Congress passed legislation to ensure that this landmark was known by its proper name, Hoover Dam.

Aside from its remarkable features, Hoover Dam stands as proof of the will of the American people during the 1930s. This period, known as the Great Depression, was a time when many people were out of work. The construction of Hoover Dam contributed to a spirit of hope during a time of great trouble. It also provided many with employment.

Today Hoover Dam is one of the Southwest's most photographed landmarks! It is appreciated not only for its immensity and technological achievements, but also for its symbolic value. It was a remarkable achievement during a difficult time in America's history.

Directions: Answer the following questions on your own.

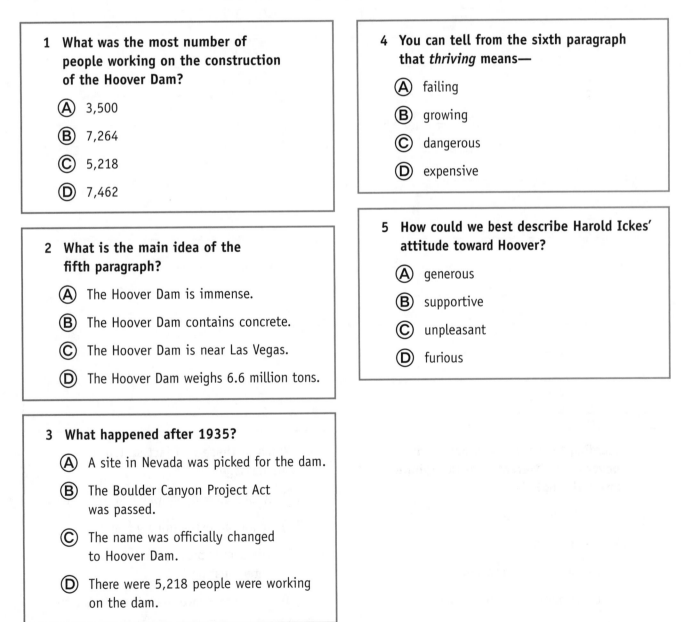

1 **What was the most number of people working on the construction of the Hoover Dam?**

Ⓐ 3,500

Ⓑ 7,264

Ⓒ 5,218

Ⓓ 7,462

2 **What is the main idea of the fifth paragraph?**

Ⓐ The Hoover Dam is immense.

Ⓑ The Hoover Dam contains concrete.

Ⓒ The Hoover Dam is near Las Vegas.

Ⓓ The Hoover Dam weighs 6.6 million tons.

3 **What happened after 1935?**

Ⓐ A site in Nevada was picked for the dam.

Ⓑ The Boulder Canyon Project Act was passed.

Ⓒ The name was officially changed to Hoover Dam.

Ⓓ There were 5,218 people were working on the dam.

4 **You can tell from the sixth paragraph that** *thriving* **means—**

Ⓐ failing

Ⓑ growing

Ⓒ dangerous

Ⓓ expensive

5 **How could we best describe Harold Ickes' attitude toward Hoover?**

Ⓐ generous

Ⓑ supportive

Ⓒ unpleasant

Ⓓ furious

6 Explain why the Hoover Dam was constructed.

_____

_____

_____

_____

_____

_____

_____

_____

_____

_____

_____

_____

_____

_____

_____

_____

_____

_____

_____

_____

_____

_____

_____

_____

7 According to the passage, how is the Hoover Dam different from the Empire State Building?

Ⓐ It is located in Utah.

Ⓑ It employs many workers.

Ⓒ It contains more concrete.

Ⓓ It was built during the 1930s.

8 Which of these is a fact stated in this passage?

Ⓐ A railroad and highway had to be built.

Ⓑ It was an extraordinary feat.

Ⓒ The dam is proof of America's determination.

Ⓓ A visit to Hoover Dam is worth the trip.

9 How might things have been different if the Hoover Dam had not been built?

_____

_____

_____

_____

_____

_____

_____

10 There is enough information in the passage to conclude that—

Ⓐ many people think the dam is a beautiful sight

Ⓑ there was no opposition to changing the dam's name

Ⓒ the construction of the dam was a very complicated task

Ⓓ construction of the dam made little difference in the Southwest

11 The fact that the Boulder Canyon Project Act was passed means that—

Ⓐ the city of Las Vegas was growing very rapidly

Ⓑ the people in the Southwest could not agree on the project

Ⓒ politicians felt there wasn't enough popular support for the law

Ⓓ several states saw a need to share the waters of the Colorado River

12 What is the author's purpose for writing this passage?

Ⓐ to encourage people to visit the dam

Ⓑ to express support for the entire project

Ⓒ to explain the growth of cities in Nevada

Ⓓ to give a brief history of the Hoover Dam

13 To find information about the Hoover Dam you should first look in—

Ⓐ an almanac

Ⓑ an encyclopedia

Ⓒ the newspaper

Ⓓ a science book

14 Where is Hoover Dam?

Ⓐ in a valley

Ⓑ in the desert

Ⓒ near the ocean

Ⓓ in the mountains

Selection 2 | Directions: Read the passage below and answer the questions that follow.

Mount Rushmore National Memorial

Mount Rushmore National Memorial is considered a "must see" by many tourists. These carvings of the likenesses of four presidents are located in the Black Hills of South Dakota. They are so huge that the head of George Washington is over 60 feet high. That is as tall as a five-story building! The following timeline shows some of the major events in the history of this amazing work.

1868   The Sioux Tribe and the United States government sign a treaty. It gives the Sioux permanent property rights in the Black Hills of South Dakota. The area has always been considered a sacred area by this Native American tribe.

1874   Lt. Col. George A. Custer leads an expedition that discovers gold in the Black Hills. The news brings huge numbers of prospectors into the region. The Sioux are forced to give up their land and relocate to nearby areas. This results in conflicts between the Sioux and the U.S. government in South Dakota. Custer is killed in the battle of Little Big Horn in 1876.

1924   Gutzon Borglum (1867-1941) is contacted about carving faces of famous people of the West, including Native Americans, into rock formations in the Black Hills. He is well known for having carved a bust of Abraham Lincoln. It was displayed in the White House when Theodore Roosevelt was president.

1925   Borglum arrives in the Black Hills. He selects Mount Rushmore as the best site for the carving. To attract national interest, it is decided that he will carve the likenesses of George Washington, Thomas Jefferson, Theodore Roosevelt, and Abraham Lincoln. He starts to plan for the *infrastructure* needed to support the project. Eventually he builds 45 ramps and a stairway of 506 steps. These are used to transport workers and supplies to the top of the mountain.

1927   Borglum and his workers begin to dynamite and drill into the surface of Mount Rushmore. Although Borglum is in charge, he is often away from the site. He travels to Washington to get more money, and works on other projects around the world.

1930   On July 4th, the head of George Washington is dedicated. The workers believe Borglum to be a demanding employer. South Dakota sometimes has extremely hot summers and cold, stormy winters. But he expects workers to be on the site every morning at 7:30 no matter what the weather conditions are.

1931   There are problems with the carving of Jefferson. The stone is not strong enough to stand the constant drilling and explosions.

1933   Lincoln Borglum (1912-1986), Gutzon's son, arrives to work at the site. A new location is chosen for Jefferson's head. It is to the left of Washington's likeness. The previous work on Jefferson is blasted away. Drill holes are filled with dynamite, which is then detonated. Many times it is difficult to control the blast. After the blast, workers remove the rubble. It's difficult and dangerous work.

1935 A suitable site is located for Roosevelt's head and the work begins. A crack in the lip of Jefferson is repaired. After the detailed work is finished, compressed air hoses are used to blow away the dust.

1936 On August 30, President Franklin Roosevelt arrives for the dedication ceremony for the head of Jefferson.

1937 On September 17, the head of Abraham Lincoln is dedicated in a ceremony. Women's rights advocates want Susan B. Anthony's head to be included on Mount Rushmore. A bill is introduced. After lengthy debate and intense opposition, the bill is defeated in Congress.

1938 The work now concentrates on the completion of the likeness of Roosevelt. The details on Washington's head are also being finalized.

1939 The head of Theodore Roosevelt is dedicated. Lighting is added to enhance the display at night. The Sioux chief, Chief Henry Standing Bear, contacts a sculptor, Korczak Ziolkowski (1908-1992). He wants him to carve a memorial to the Sioux. Ziolkowski buys a nearby mountain and begins to carve a sculpture of Chief Crazy Horse. This warrior led the Sioux in their fight to save their lands. Even though Ziolkowski died in 1988, his family continues his work. It is dedicated in 1998.

1941 Gutzon Borglum dies on March 6th. His son is asked to complete the work, which is finished on October 31.

2002 More than 2.5 million people visit the site, which has been called the largest work of art on Earth.

Directions: Answer the following questions on your own.

1 Who was Korczak Ziolkowski?

(A) a senator

(B) a famous leader

(C) a sculptor

(D) Borglum's stepson

2 How could you summarize the events of 1933?

(A) Holes had to be drilled and filled with dynamite.

(B) Many laborers were needed to complete the work.

(C) Gutzon's son, Lincoln Borglum arrived in South Dakota.

(D) The work was very difficult and extremely dangerous.

3 According to the passage, when were problems with the likeness of Jefferson first encountered?

(A) before Lincoln Borglum arrived in South Dakota

(B) after Ziolkowski begins work on the sculpture of Chief Crazy Horse

(C) before Borglum went to Washington to ask for more funding

(D) after Franklin Roosevelt participated in the dedication ceremony

4 The word *infrastructure* in the 1925 entry means—

(A) funding

(B) buildings

(C) detailed blueprints and diagrams

(D) constructions for transportation

5 Which word best describes Gutzon Borglum?

Ⓐ lazy

Ⓑ thrifty

Ⓒ determined

Ⓓ sympathetic

6 Explain why there was a debate about Mount Rushmore in Congress.

_____

_____

_____

_____

_____

_____

_____

_____

_____

_____

_____

_____

_____

7 According to the passage, how was Gutzon Borglum different from Korczak Ziolkowski?

Ⓐ Borglum was a demanding boss, while Ziolkowski was much gentler.

Ⓑ Borglum did his work in South Dakota, and Ziolkowski worked in Washington.

Ⓒ Borglum carved Presidents, and Ziolkowski carved a Native American leader.

Ⓓ Borglum died a rich man, and Ziolkowski never became wealthy.

8 Which of the following is NOT a fact?

Ⓐ Gutzon Borglum died in 1941.

Ⓑ In 1868 the Sioux signed a treaty.

Ⓒ Mount Rushmore is considered a "must see."

Ⓓ There are millions of visitors each year.

9 Which of the following would Borglum probably have done if he had lived longer?

Ⓐ campaigned to be a Senator

Ⓑ retired in the Black Hills area

Ⓒ vacationed around the world

Ⓓ started work on another project

10 Why do so many people visit Mount Rushmore?

Ⓐ Americans love to learn about history.

Ⓑ South Dakota is a great place to visit.

Ⓒ It is an important American symbol.

Ⓓ Borglum was a famous American sculptor.

11 How can you tell from the passage that the work on Mount Rushmore was dangerous?

_____

_____

_____

_____

_____

_____

_____

_____

_____

_____

_____

_____

_____

_____

_____

_____

_____

_____

_____

_____

12 This passage was most likely written to—

Ⓐ persuade

Ⓑ entertain

Ⓒ inform

Ⓓ inspire

13 In which section of the library is this passage most likely to be found?

Ⓐ History

Ⓑ Biography

Ⓒ Science

Ⓓ Travel

14 Where is Mount Rushmore located?

Ⓐ The Rocky Mountains

Ⓑ The Pacific Northwest

Ⓒ The Great Plains

Ⓓ The Appalachian Mountains

Portland Head Light

My grandfather has always been fascinated with lighthouses. Learning about them and then building delicate models are his favorite hobbies. He also loves to read the journals and diaries that describe the hard lives the lighthouse keepers and their families led. Their dedication and heroics saved many lives over the years. He's got me interested, too! I've read as many books on lighthouses and their families as I can find. And we shopped for supplies, so that I can build my first miniature lighthouse.

We live on Long Island, New York where thousands of pleasure and commercial boats ply the waters that surround us. Lighthouses continue to help navigation in this area. Unlike years ago, however, most are now computerized.

Although we've visited many of our local lights, my grandfather wanted to visit the famous Portland Head Light in Cape Elizabeth, Maine. For his seventieth birthday, the family made this dream come true. They booked him on a lighthouse tour of southern Maine, and I was to be his traveling companion!

When we arrived in August, I was surprised to see that the Portland Head Light and its Keepers' Quarters were located in a park called Fort Williams Park. It was filled with families picnicking, biking, playing soccer, flying kites, and exploring some historic forts on the grounds. For us, however, the real attraction was the light itself.

It looked so majestic standing on a high bluff, surrounded on three sides by the cold, clear waters of Casco Bay. Before we even entered the lighthouse grounds with our guide, the three of us sat on a grassy hill overlooking the compound. Dramatic waves pounded the rocky shoreline, sending salty spray high into the air. We could feel, even taste the sea. Our guide told us that dangerous currents surge through the area.

We entered the museum, looked at the exhibits, and spent some time reading the story of the three-masted *bark,* which was named the *Annie C. Maguire.* On Christmas Eve in 1886, it crashed on the rocks, just yards from the front door of the lighthouse. The captain and crew were saved by the ingenuity of the keeper, his family, and volunteers who rigged an ordinary ladder as a gangplank between the shore and the wreck. As I read the story of the rescue, I recognized the courage that was displayed that day.

As I read on, a picture emerged of the difficult times these families endured. Although Portland Head Light is on the mainland in Cape Elizabeth, other lighthouses are located on remote islands. Families could not leave the island for weeks at a time if the weather did not cooperate. Often keepers and their families grew their own vegetables and raised animals to eat since they were not always able to go to a store. Often, there was no electricity, and families had to know how to handle medical problems, since a doctor was not "around the corner."

When the keeper found it necessary to row to the mainland, he may not have been able to return if the weather and waves became too severe. The keeper's wife, therefore, had to know how to take care of the light and handle many emergencies. When you read some of the journals, you recognize the bravery shown by these women.

I was also intrigued by the workings of the light. In 1791 the original 72-foot tower, later raised an additional 20 feet, was lit with 16 whale oil lamps. One of the main duties of the keeper was to haul the oil up many steps to keep the lamp lit. What a reassuring sight it must have been against the black night on the edge of the dark land! A portion of the beautiful Fresnel lens in use from 1865 to 1958 was on display. I'm sure it saved many lives.

After our guide left us for the day, we walked along the park's trails and continued to enjoy the views of Portland Head Light. Before we left, we made sure to visit the rock that the *Annie C. Maguire* hit that fateful night. On the rock is written the name of the ship and the date of the wreck. After all I had learned, I could almost envision that Christmas Eve long ago. This was a visit I won't soon forget.

PART B: The 14 Essential Skills for Reading Success — *All Together*

Directions: Answer the following questions on your own.

1 Which park surrounds the Portland Head Light?

ⓐ Cape Elizabeth Park

ⓑ Fort Williams Park

ⓒ Portland Park

ⓓ Annie Maguire Park

2 Another good title for this passage would be—

ⓐ "A Lighthouse Lover's Dream Trip"

ⓑ "The Amazing Fresnel Lens"

ⓒ "My Wonderful Grandfather"

ⓓ "Dangerous Shipwrecks and Rescues"

3 Which of the following happened before the author and his grandfather visited Maine?

ⓐ They saw people flying kites and having picnics.

ⓑ They saw a portion of the Fresnel Lens on display.

ⓒ They visited some of the lighthouses on Long Island.

ⓓ They took photos of Casco Bay.

4 The author of the passage uses the word *bark* to mean

ⓐ a rowboat

ⓑ a sharp tone

ⓒ a sailing ship

ⓓ a tree covering

5 From what we learn of the lighthouse keeper and his family in the passage, which of the following words best describes them?

ⓐ lazy

ⓑ mean

ⓒ friendly

ⓓ dedicated

6 Why did his family send the author's grandfather to Maine?

ⓐ He needed a rest.

ⓑ He loved lighthouses.

ⓒ He wanted to go sailing.

ⓓ He enjoyed eating lobster.

7 According to the passage, what is one way Long Island and Cape Elizabeth are similar?

ⓐ They are both in Maine.

ⓑ They both have lighthouses.

ⓒ They are both on Casco Bay.

ⓓ They both have exhibits about the Portland Head Light.

8 Which of these is an opinion stated in this passage?

ⓐ It looked so majestic standing on a high bluff.

ⓑ On Christmas Eve in 1886, it struck a ledge.

ⓒ Fort Williams Park has picnic areas.

ⓓ Lighthouses continue to help navigation.

9 What will the author and his grandfather probably tell their family after they return home from their visit to the Portland Head Light?

_____

_____

_____

_____

_____

_____

_____

_____

_____

_____

_____

_____

_____

_____

_____

_____

_____

_____

_____

10 What generalization can you make based on this passage?

Ⓐ All shorelines are dangerous.

Ⓑ Maine is a great place to visit.

Ⓒ Lighthouses are still important.

Ⓓ Lighthouses are no longer needed.

11 Cape Elizabeth is best described as—

Ⓐ arid

Ⓑ scenic

Ⓒ noisy

Ⓓ deserted

12 In the fifth paragraph, the author sets the tone for the rest of the passage by—

(A) explaining why they did not visit the forts

(B) telling how the author and his grandfather sat on the hill

(C) explaining how the lighthouse is surrounded by the ocean

(D) describing some of the activities available in Fort Williams Park

13 You might expect to find this passage in a book titled—

(A) *Lighthouses of Long Island*

(B) *The History of the Fresnel Lens*

(C) *Lighthouses of America*

(D) *How to Build a Lighthouse*

14 Why do you think the Portland Head Light was built on a cliff?

A STOP ON THE FREEDOM TRAIL

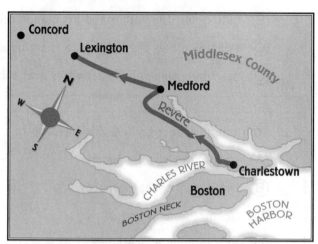

One of the historic sites on Boston's Freedom Trail is the Old North Church. In his poem, *Paul Revere's Ride,* Longfellow described what happened in 1775 when Robert Newman, the caretaker, hung two lanterns in the church tower. This let Paul Revere know that the British troops were going to row across the Charles River and head northwest. They were not going to march down Boston Neck and then north to Concord.

On the ride to Lexington, Revere spread the word that the troops were on the move. As he left that town to continue on to Concord, Revere was arrested by the British. After being released, Revere started back to Lexington and was present for part of the battle on the next day.

Longfellow wrote the poem in 1861, long after the event. He was more interested in telling about Revere's achievement than in giving a factual account of the event. Not all the details in the poem are accurate.

Illustration courtesy of the Library of Congress.

Paul Revere's Ride
by Henry Wadsworth Longfellow (1807-1882)

1   Listen, my children, and you shall hear
Of the midnight ride of Paul Revere,
On the eighteenth of April, in Seventy-five;
Hardly a man is now alive
Who remembers that famous day and year.

2   He said to his friend, "If the British march
By land or sea from the town to-night,
Hang a lantern aloft in the belfry arch
Of the North Church tower as a signal light,--
One, if by land, and two, if by sea;
And I on the opposite shore will be,
Ready to ride and spread the alarm
Through every Middlesex village and farm,
For the country folk to be up and to arm."

3   Then he said, "Good-night!" and with muffled oar
Silently rowed to the Charlestown shore,
Just as the moon rose over the bay,
Where swinging wide at her moorings lay
The Somerset, British man-of-war;
A phantom ship, with each mast and spar
Across the moon like a prison bar,
And a huge black hulk, that was magnified
By its own reflection in the tide.

4   Meanwhile, his friend, through alley and street,
Wanders and watches with eager ears,
Till in the silence around him he hears
The muster of men at the barrack door,
The sound of arms, and the tramp of feet,
And the measured tread of the grenadiers,
Marching down to their boats on the shore.

5   Then he climbed the tower of the Old North Church,
By the wooden stairs, with stealthy tread,
To the belfry-chamber overhead,
And startled the pigeons from their perch
On the sombre rafters, that round him made
Masses and moving shapes of shade,--
By the trembling ladder, steep and tall,
To the highest window in the wall,
Where he paused to listen and look down
A moment on the roofs of the town,
And the moonlight flowing over all.

6 Beneath, in the churchyard, lay the dead,
In their night encampment on the hill,
Wrapped in silence so deep and still
That he could hear, like a sentinel's tread,
The watchful night-wind, as it went
Creeping along from tent to tent,
And seeming to whisper, "All is well!"
A moment only he feels the spell
Of the place and the hour, and the secret dread
Of the lonely belfry and the dead;
For suddenly all his thoughts are *bent*
On a shadowy something far away,
Where the river widens to meet the bay,--
A line of black that bends and floats
On the rising tide, like a bridge of boats.

7 Meanwhile, impatient to mount and ride,
Booted and spurred, with a heavy stride
On the opposite shore walked Paul Revere.
Now he patted his horse's side,
Now gazed at the landscape far and near,
Then, impetuous, stamped the earth,
And turned and tightened his saddle-girth;
But mostly he watched with eager search
The belfry tower of the Old North Church,
As it rose above the graves on the hill,
Lonely and spectral and sombre and still.
And lo! as he looks, on the belfry's height
A glimmer, and then a gleam of light!
He springs to the saddle, the bridle he turns,
But lingers and gazes, till full on his sight
A second lamp in the belfry burns!

8 A hurry of hoofs in a village street,
A shape in the moonlight, a bulk in the dark,
And beneath, from the pebbles, in passing, a spark
Struck out by a steed flying fearless and fleet:
That was all! And yet, through the gloom and the light,
The fate of a nation was riding that night;
And the spark struck out by that steed, in his flight,
Kindled the land into flame with its heat.

9 He has left the village and mounted the steep,
And beneath him, tranquil and broad and deep,
Is the Mystic, meeting the ocean tides;
And under the alders that skirt its edge,
Now soft on the sand, now loud on the ledge,
Is heard the tramp of his steed as he rides.

10 It was twelve by the village clock,
When he crossed the bridge into Medford town.
He heard the crowing of the cock,
And the barking of the farmer's dog,
And felt the damp of the river fog,
That rises after the sun goes down.

11 It was one by the village clock,
When he galloped into Lexington.
He saw the gilded weathercock
Swim in the moonlight as he passed,
And the meeting-house windows, blank and bare,
Gaze at him with a spectral glare,
As if they already stood aghast
At the bloody work they would look upon.

12 It was two by the village clock,
When he came to the bridge in Concord town.
He heard the bleating of the flock,
And the twitter of birds among the trees,
And felt the breath of the morning breeze
Blowing over the meadows brown.
And one was safe and asleep in his bed
Who at the bridge would be first to fall,
Who that day would be lying dead,
Pierced by a British musket-ball.

13 You know the rest. In the books you have read
How the British Regulars fired and fled,---
How the farmers gave them ball for ball,
From behind each fence and farm-yard wall,
Chasing the red-coats down the lane,
Then crossing the fields to emerge again
Under the trees at the turn of the road,
And only pausing to fire and load.

14 So through the night rode Paul Revere;
And so through the night went his cry of alarm
To every Middlesex village and farm,--
A cry of defiance and not of fear,
A voice in the darkness, a knock at the door,
And a word that shall echo forevermore!
For, borne on the night-wind of the Past,
Through all our history, to the last,
In the hour of darkness and peril and need,
The people will waken and listen to hear
The hurrying hoof-beats of that steed,
And the midnight message of Paul Revere.

Directions: Answer the following questions on your own.

1   **Read these lines from the poem.**

   "It was two by the village clock, When he came to the bridge in Concord town."

   These lines show that—

   Ⓐ the poem has no rhyming pattern

   Ⓑ Paul Revere was an excellent rider

   Ⓒ the poet admires Revere's determination

   Ⓓ the poet did not base the entire poem on facts

2   **What is the main idea that is expressed in the sixth stanza of this poem?**

   Ⓐ Revere feels very alone in the belfry.

   Ⓑ Revere's friend sees that the British boats are leaving Boston.

   Ⓒ Revere's friend is afraid because the church is near the graveyard.

   Ⓓ British soldiers are building a long, black bridge across the water.

3   **What did Paul Revere do after he saw a light in the belfry and got on his horse?**

   Ⓐ He started his ride to Lexington.

   Ⓑ He crossed the river to Charleston.

   Ⓒ He waited to see if a second lantern would be lit.

   Ⓓ He watched British soldiers marching to their boats.

4   **Read the following lines from the sixth stanza in the poem.**

   "For suddenly all his thoughts are bent On a shadowy something far away,"

   What does the word _bent_ mean as it is used here.

   Ⓐ focused

   Ⓑ ended

   Ⓒ shattered

   Ⓓ delayed

5   **Which words best describes the mood in the belfry-chamber on that night?**

   Ⓐ cheerful and bright

   Ⓑ quiet and serene

   Ⓒ lonely and tense

   Ⓓ noisy and crowded

6 Why didn't Revere let the people of Concord know that the British troops were coming?

_____

_____

_____

_____

_____

_____

_____

_____

_____

_____

_____

_____

_____

_____

_____

_____

_____

_____

_____

_____

_____

_____

_____

_____

7 How was the experience of Paul Revere and his friend the same on the evening night of April 18, 1775?

(A) They both saw a gilded weathercock in the moonlight.

(B) They both tried to see what was happening at the soldiers' barracks.

(C) They both waited to find out if the soldiers were crossing the river.

(D) They both looked down at the roofs of the town in the moonlight.

8 Read the last stanza of the poem. Is it opinion or fact? Explain your answer.

_____

_____

_____

_____

_____

_____

_____

_____

_____

_____

_____

_____

_____

_____

_____

_____

_____

_____

_____

_____

_____

9 After Paul Revere's friend sent the signal, he probably—

Ⓐ joined the grenadiers for a late dinner

Ⓑ was happy because he had been helpful

Ⓒ was worried about what would happen next

Ⓓ rode to Lexington, so he could see the battle

10 Based on the information in the poem, the weather that night was—

Ⓐ foggy

Ⓑ cold

Ⓒ hot

Ⓓ clear

11 Based on the map, what may be one reason that the British decided to row across the river instead of marching across Boston Neck?

_____

_____

_____

_____

_____

_____

_____

_____

_____

_____

_____

_____

_____

_____

_____

_____

_____

12 What is the author's purpose for writing this poem?

Ⓐ to encourage people to report troop movements

Ⓑ to provide a factual account of Paul Revere's ride

Ⓒ to retell the story of an important historical event

Ⓓ to remind people that it's important to have good friends

13 If you want to read more of Longfellow's work, you should get—

Ⓐ an almanac

Ⓑ a biography

Ⓒ a book of poems

Ⓓ a history book

14 The battle at Lexington was fought during—

Ⓐ the Civil War

Ⓑ the Korean War

Ⓒ the American Revolution

Ⓓ the French Revolution

Theme Questions

Directions: The second theme of Section 2 was, "Remarkable American Achievements." Answer these questions. They are about the four Theme B selections you just read.

---

1 Where on the Mount Rushmore timeline would the completion of Hoover Dam appear?

(A) before Theodore Roosevelt was president

(B) before Gutzon Borglum built a stairway to help the workers on the project

(C) between the repair of Jefferson's lip and the rejection of the inclusion of Susan B. Anthony

(D) between the dedication of George Washington's head and the arrival of Lincoln Borglum in South Dakota

---

2 How do the four selections support the theme, "Remarkable American Achievements"?

_____

_____

_____

_____

_____

_____

_____

_____

_____

_____

_____

_____

_____

_____

_____

_____

_____

_____

3 Feelings of admiration are expressed in "Portland Head Light" and "Paul Revere's Ride." How do the authors demonstrate these feelings?

_____

_____

_____

_____

_____

_____

_____

_____

_____

_____

_____

_____

_____

_____

_____

_____

_____

_____

_____

_____

_____

_____

_____

_____

_____

_____

_____

_____

_____

Notes